James Bowen Everhart

Miscellanies

James Bowen Everhart
Miscellanies
ISBN/EAN: 9783337418052

Printed in Europe, USA, Canada, Australia, Japan

Cover: Foto ©Thomas Meinert / pixelio.de

More available books at **www.hansebooks.com**

MISCELLANIES.

BY

JAMES B. EVERHART.

" Frustra laborat, qui omnibus placere studet."

WEST CHESTER:
EDWARD F. JAMES,
1862.

Entered according to Act of Congress, in the year 1862, by
JAMES B. EVERHART,
In the Clerk's Office of the District Court of the United States, in and for the Eastern District of Pennsylvania.

JAMES, Printer,
West Chester, Pa.

CLARK, Binder,
West Chester, Pa

TO THE

HON. CHARLES MINER,

AUTHOR OF THE "HISTORY OF WYOMING," &C.

Your talents and virtues, which have given you

LITERARY REPUTATION, POLITICAL HONORS, AND UNIVERSAL ESTEEM

And which have been rendered still more attractive to me, by

Early Associations,

AND YOUR LONG, UNBROKEN FRIENDSHIP WITH MY FATHER,

Induce the liberty I take in dedicating to you these discursive papers.

THE AUTHOR.

PREFACE.

The following pages, containing essays, addresses and personal reminiscences of the author, could hardly be recommended by apologies for their publication. It may, however, be suggested that if the articles be without interest, they are generally short—that if the subjects be not new, they are at least varied—that if the descriptions be imperfect, they are not fictitious—and that to no part of the work can be attributed an unseemly tendency, or an unworthy purpose.

WEST CHESTER, 1862.

CONTENTS.

	PAGE
ABBOTSFORD AND MELROSE	37
ALEXANDRIA AND CAIRO	148
ALPS TO PISA	94
ATHENS	215
AYR	43
AGRICULTURAL ADDRESS—1855	229
BALLOONS	255
BERLIN	200
BEER TO TYRE	195
BETHLEHEM	189
BEDOUIN AND HIS FRIENDS	164
BROUGHAM, LORD	40
BULL FIGHT IN MADRID	128
CHOATE, RUFUS, REMINISCENCE	1
CHESTER, SOMETIMES CALLED WEST CHESTER, (ENGLAND)	12
CONSTANTINOPLE	207
CRYSTAL PALACE	289
DESERT	158
DOG BOZ	98
EASTER FESTIVAL	178
ESCURIAL	126
FLORENCE	226
GOLDSMITH, OLIVER	294
GUIDES	246
GERMAN BARON, A VISIT TO	163
HOLLAND	269

INDUSTRY, MISAPPLIED	45
IRELAND, TRIP IN	57
JERUSALEM	167
JOE	84
JORDAN ROBBERS	181
JEWS	185
LOCH LOMOND AND LOCH KATRINE	19
LETTERS OF CREDIT	220
MAIDEN SPEECH	280
NILE	151
NAPOLEON, LOUIS	285
NAPLES	119
ORATION, 22D OF FEBRUARY, 1848	186
ORIENT	133
PARIS	68
POPE, VISIT TO THE	116
PASSPORTS, CUSTOM HOUSES AND QUARANTINE	199
RACES AT ASCOT	14
RHINE	275
RIDE ON THE PRAIRIES	90
ROME	109
SHAM SMUGGLERS	62
SECTS, RELIGIOUS, IN JERUSALEM	192
SIMPLON PASS OVER THE ALPS	88
STORY, JUDGE	72
SULTAN ABDUL MEDJID	211
SWITZERLAND	80
VENICE	243
VESUVIUS AND POMPEII	122
VIENNA	250
WINE VAULTS IN LONDON	5
WOMEN	21

MISCELLANIES.

REMINISCENCE OF RUFUS CHOATE.

One sultry fourth of July, on the famous field of Concord, a huge canvas tent shaded ten thousand partisans of that gifted leader, who was destined like Moses, to lead his hosts to the land he could not reach himself.

Numerous men of mark sat on an elevated platform, eating like other hungry people; but whose organism, unlike theirs, would transmute the food by a sort of alchemy, into thoughts which move the world.

There was Webster, universally hailed the defender of the Constitution—with the fresh honor of diplomatic triumph on his massy brows—with the consciousness of matchless eloquence upon his scornful lips—coming, as it were, like another Achilles, to cast dismay upon the foe, by his majestic presence.

There were the benevolent features and bald head of Abbott Lawrence—the great merchant, and the fine gentleman—representing the aristocracy of commerce, the American patronage of learning, and the princely hospitality of Boston.

There was Horace Greeley, with hair and clothes as light as his complexion; whose plain demeanor, homely gestures, and drawling elocution marred the vast information and vigorous style of the editorial tribune.

There was another person whom I did not know. He had a sad, thoughtful face, half poetical, half philosophical, such as you see in the pictures of Lamartine. He was nervous. He ate but little. He pushed his fingers through his raven curls. His dreamy oriental eyes glanced from earth to heaven. Light and shade flitted alternately across his brow. He moved about on his seat. He seemed excited with deep feeling. So you might suppose the priestess appeared when about to utter the oracle; or the prophet on the point of proclaiming the vision.

The Chairman, Mr. Hoar, addressed him:—"I trust our senatorial friend will allow us to ask him, 'Watchman, what of the night?'"

Tumultuous applause greeted the unknown figure with cheers for Choate, as he rose to answer.

A tall man, he lifted himself up to his full height, pale and trembling with emotion, he stretched forth his arm. Amidst a silence like night, with a look radiant of genius, and in a voice eloquent as an angel's, he exclaimed: "The morning cometh! Thank God! the morning cometh!" An exordium, so prompt and happy, thrilled the innumerable crowd like magic. Subdued murmurs of delight escaped them, and compelled him to pause. As he proceeded he seemed to sway them by a sort of fascination, they hung with parted lips upon his accents, captive to every thought he uttered. Such brilliant power, such genial sensibility, dazzled the imagination, warmed the blood, filled the soul. His wit, his pathos, his sarcasm, his imagery, were all effective. You could read the deep indignation on all faces, when he referred to the Texas land jobbers speculating in war. Men shook with laughter, when in an irresistable manner, he spoke of Mr. Polk's name not having been written between Orion and the Pleiades, and the perplexity of his friends in proving his opinions by witnesses and affidavits. They listened with breathless admiration, when he alluded to the fitness of the assembly then and there; and recalled the first fierce struggle and the generous bloodshed of those heroic martyrs, whom the angels in chariots of fire led on to victory and to heaven. And few were unmoved when, turning from the past and the dead, he pointed to the Revolutionary veterans near him, covered with the honored marks of war and time, ready to renew their patriotic vows, and consecrate their closing days, as they had their best, on the altar of their country.

In conclusion he referred in complimentary terms to Greeley for his advocacy of a protective tariff, and said of it, that it is a principle native to the soil, and as essential as the ballot. That labor is the true foundation of liberty—that it must forge the national weapons and weave the national colors. That while liberty sheds its hallowed light over our institutions, labor lends its sturdy arm for their support in peace, and for their defence in war.

He ceased—but the effect of his oratory was permanent. No one could forget his impressive emphasis, which varied through all the notes of tuneful sounds—his pictorial words which seemed to make thought sensible to sight—his impassioned logic which glowed through his periods with the energy of fire.

Sometimes he spoke with such insinuating force that you might suppose of him as of Pericles, that the goddess of persuasion dwelt upon his lips. And sometimes he displayed as much vehemence as if the furies had roused him to ecstasy.

Occasionally his speech had the delicious sweetness of some one gentle instrument of music. And occasionally, it had the swelling grandeur and crashing thunders of the orchestra.

WINE VAULTS IN LONDON.

An English official, born within the cockney precincts of Bowbells, invited me and others to St. Catherine's docks. We boarded one of the small steamers which ply between the bridges for a penny a head. We glided down the yellow Thames, turbid with the drainage of the city, by barges and skiffs, palaces and churches, warehouses and markets, prisons and gardens.

Arrived at the docks, we looked over the vast basins, in which one hundred and fifty ships can safely ride. We passed through the lofty buildings, filled with imports from all quarters. We went down into those vaulted chambers, which occupy acres with avenues and alcoholic fluids.

A journey below the earth's surface seems to inspire a feeling akin to dread. I had experienced it going into the mines, where the collier, with a lamp in the middle of his forehead, recalls the single eye of Cyclops —and as I entered the intricate alleys of the catacombs, where the early Christians hid from Roman persecution, worshiped and buried—as I crossed the saltpetre threshold of the mammoth cave, with its dark river and blind fishes, and gorgeous crystalizations—as I descended the spiral path of Joseph's well in Cairo—as I ventured into the dusty aisles of the old Egyptian tombs, marvelous with paintings—and others have told of their distrust, as they went down amongst the coral colonnades, which, beneath the keels of navies, form the silent cities of the ocean.

And though our descent was as easy as that to Avernus, and our errand as attractive as that which tempted Orpheus, and our guide as skilful as the shade that directed Dante—yet the palpable darkness, scarcely disturbed by our single candle, shining like "a good deed in a naughty world," and the cool dank atmosphere breathing on us, still conveyed the impression of mystery and doubt. Yet down we wandered, by rows of hogsheads, by walls of bottles, by stacks of demijohns, filled with infinite liquors. They were gathered from different markets and distant lands—from beyond the oceans and the mountains; from the pleasant south; from the icy north; from the log stills of the prairies; from the rude presses of the east. There were the treasures of luxurious climates and prodigal soils—the juices of delicious fruits; the essence of corn and cane; the flavor of peaches, juniper and grapes. There were the "fiery Hollands," West India rum, Bourbon whiskey, and the true Cogniac—elements of those ingenious mixtures, which, under the names of "schnapps," "punch" and "smashers," are so prevalent and popular above ground.

There were wines of various vintages and brands—harsh and mellow, sweet and tart, light and heavy; some as famous as the old Falernian of Horace, as the Samian cup of Anacreon, as Homer's Maronean.

There were thousands of the Hock which Byron loved —tuns of that fine port of Tennyson, "whose father grape grew fat on Lusitanian summers;" pipes of that rare Madeira which Holmes says,

"Shows how delusion comes;"

great casks of what Hunt calls "glorious claret;" uncounted baskets of Ainsworth's "cold champagne." Thus surrounded, we were persuaded to investigate those luxuries, which could make the hour delicious with song and laughter; which could transfigure the dim walls of the cellar into some brilliant cave of Arabian story, or the green vault of Dresden, with its diamonds.

So, beneath the floating drapery of cobwebs and the fluttering wings of bats, we sat down amidst the treasures and the altars of the rosy god. We could not then forget how universal is his rule, how potential is the sceptre which he sways. No isothermal lines, no geographical boundaries, no physical prowess, no boasted ciilvizations limit his power. It reaches court and cot, town and district, ship and strand, trade and letters, misfortune and amusement. Everywhere the genial fluid fascinates with its beauty of color, its beaded motion, its thrilling taste. It often controls more than reason, is more insinuating than flattery, more exciting than ambition, stronger than love, and sweeter than life. It offers to re-animate the faculties of age, to resist the assaults of disease, to wash away, like Lethe, the poignant memory of disasters. It promises a spur to genius, invocation to charity, to uphold the energies in the harvest and in the battle, to heighten the joys of the feast and the fireside. It pretends to quench thirst, to cool the blood, to expel the biting frost, to give peace to conscience, and repose to care. Did it not make Falstaff witty, and Caliban hospitable? Did it not sustain the fancy of Sheridan, the logic of Pitt, the song of Burns, the tragic muse of Æschylus, the Latin speech of Sir Thomas More?

It has been from immemorial time the pledge of health, of friendship and of faith. We read how libations of wine pleased the nostrils of the gods. That pagans called it the nectar of heaven; and Christians, the tears of Jesus. That it was the subject of the first miracle, and the last sacrament. That it entered into the mysteries of Eleusis and the banquet of Plato. That Paul suggested its use in sickness, and Seneca, in vigor. That on account of it a Sultan conquered Cyprus. That an ancient custom adorned the drunkard with a crown of gold. That Cyrus deemed himself fitter than his rival for a king, for being a deeper drinker.

But with all our prepossessions in favor of the generous vine juice; notwithstanding its prescriptive virtues and popular praises—when the various specimens of it were brought us for experiment; when we saw it mantling in the glass; arrayed in all its enchantments; flashing with bright hues; lifting itself like flames—we could not but remember the graphic image of Solomon, and the repentant speech of Cassio. We thought how it may have sweetened the apple which cheated Eve! how it induced the shame of Noah, and the crime of Lot! how it blasted the life of Poe! made Swift a lunatic! Savage a murderer! Porson a brute! How it disgusted Sparta with its victims, and deposed Cleomenes from his throne!

But when we tasted it, and like Philoxenus, craved a deeper throat to prolong the sensation! when we enjoyed its delicious contact with the palate! felt its ravishing warmth permeating through the system! moving the blood with exhilarated speed! giving new fancies to the mind, new light to the eye, new tones to the lips! When we saw its influence reflected in the expression of one another; unfolding our charities; warming our sympathies; drawing us like love together —we, too, like many others, began to deem the bowl of Bacchus, no less than the Pierian spring, a well of inspiration.

It directed our imagination to the upper world. We recalled the scenes of busy life above us. We rang our glasses to the national airs; we perfumed the beverage with endearing sentiment; we quaffed to the glory of free rulers; to the genius of science; to the spirit of the century; to the empire of commerce; to the republic of letters; to the universal beauty of women; to the charms of the distant transatlantic. The mute old arches grew resonant with merry jests and voluptuous idyls; and the twilight gloom disappeared before the flashes of wit and the sparkles of wine.

What to us were the cellars of Hortensius; the table of Apicius; or Macaulay's "sunny halves of peaches, and brains of singing birds?" We were already realizing the Elysium of the senses. We already seemed, like the Persian Temschid, to read in the wine cup the mysteries of the past and future.

With this hour of subterranean experience, we might no longer wonder at the vast power which lay around us in repose. There was sufficient to stimulate and corrupt the age; to fill the land with mischief or with mirth. We might well muse upon its marvelous mission; its destined wide spread distribution; its various ultimate consumers! What an essential feature it would make in public and private assemblies! How conspicuous it would be in historical commemorations; in the inauguration of enterprises; in the opening of railroads; in the launching of vessels; on the birth days of benefactors; on the coronation of kings; on the election of Presidents! How it would contribute to the attractive ceremonies of marriage; to the funereal vigils of the wake; to the fantastic movements of the dance; to the boisterous pomp of parades!

How it would magnify and diminish individual fortunes! What acres and mansions it would accumulate and sweep away! It would require besides vast labor to fashion wood, clay and metal to receive it thereafter. To make vessels for it, men would be cutting the cedars of Canada; preparing the tin of Malacca; smelting the ores of Schuylkill; washing in the mines of Sacramento; diving for the pearls of India; blowing glass in Venice; tempering the earth of Staffordshire; carving the alabaster of Egypt; moulding the gutta percha of Singapore; gilding the porcelain of Sevres. In such numerous fabrics, it would be dealt out in various quantities by myriads of characters, from custom, for favor and for money. Thus scattered abroad, it would be sought as an antidote for pain; it would be denounced as a fountain of woe; it would be bowed to as a divinity; it would be fought against as a devil. It would seduce men to folly, poverty, crime and madness. It would fill streets and homes, day and night, with oaths and blows, and shame. It would supply courts with contests; jails with convicts; hospitals with patients;

cemetries with graves. It would give abundant work to philanthropist and Christian.

And though the times are better than they were, when the greatest drinker was the greatest man; when the host never left his friend until he saw him under the table; when inscriptions on tankards ordered one "not to leave a drop," and to "drink till he could not stir a foot;" when drinking guilds were all in vogue; when parsons kept the best wine; when the wassail bowl was the symbol of hospitality. Yet still in spite of experience and of lectures; in spite of societies, of churches, of newspapers, of schoolmasters; in spite of laws and politics—king alcohol still holds his own, and stands his ground, and will not die.

CHESTER, SOMETIMES CALLED WEST CHESTER, (ENGLAND).

The country from Liverpool to this place is diversified by hills and plains, by cottages and trees, and streams. The fields are inclosed by hedges, and the soil is rich in grain. The rail road banks are gay with clover and garden flowers.

Chester was called Cestria by the Latins, from castra a camp, once located here. It exhibits an odd arrangement of brick and mortar, and a deal of age, and mold, and dilapidation. It contains a great variety of ruins. They date its origin two hundred and fifty years after the deluge, and claim a grandson of Noah for its founder. They aver that a skeleton, nine feet in length was dug out of one of its streets, which connects its history with those days when there were giants. It was doubtless a town when London was a wood or morass, and before a Roman keel touched the channel. The twentieth legion of the Empire quartered here after their last battle with Boadicea. They encompassed it with a wall. They constructed elaborate roads through it. They built altars within it to their Gods. The remains of their baths, the weapons of gladiators, statues of divinities, and the coins of Emperors, taken from the soil, are still to be seen. After them the Danes, Welsh, Saxons, and Britons, contended with alternate success for the city. On the river Dee which flows around it, Edgar was once rowed by eight conquered

Kings. Close by, Harold, after the battle of Hastings, closed his life in a hermit's cell. Hither the first William came flushed with triumph; and the second Henry, after his defeat by the Welsh, to receive the homage of Malcolm of Scotland. In the Castle, the Welsh made a final submission to Edward. From the tower Charles the first beheld his defeat by Cromwell's soldiery; and the building, adorned with a curious stone mantel, is still shown where his son frolicked during the Protectorate. The city was loyal, and the cannon of the Roundheads thundered for half a year against its walls.

The streets are rectangular, and the old houses project one story over another. The Cathedral is of fine proportions, seven hundred years old. It is remarkable for the elaborate ornaments on the Bishop's throne, the choir, and the Gothic screen, and the bones and effigy of the first Earl of Chester.

St. John's church is still older, built, they say, where Ethelred saw a white hind. Within it is a sort of gallery over the pews, where the nuns, unseen, attended worship.

From the new tower, built in the 15th century, and one hundred and thirty feet high, the view is grand. There are the rivers winding around the walls, the antique city, Beeston castle, the sweeping level of green grass, the far off hills of Wales, and the illimitable expanse of the sea.

THE RACES AT ASCOT.

It was a pleasant holiday when I saw the horses run at Ascot. Other courses perhaps may attract as dense a crowd, but this one enjoys the presence of the Court. Long trains of rail cars ran full. All curious conveyances which extemporaneous necessity contrives, filled the roads. There were carts and gigs of different styles and ages, faded and out of fashion; huge baskets, rough boxes, and sections of hogheads were mounted on wheels more or less elliptical. There were large horses from the dray and plough, under the saddle and under second hand clothes—diminutive donkeys almost concealed by their riders—fancy beasts, variously crippled and colored, which had passed their prime and like some party hacks survived their friends. There were parties on foot picking their way along paths and over stiles—equipages brilliant with liveries and heraldry—the royal carriages, each drawn by four greys, with postillions and mounted grooms—all hastening forward amidst dust, noise and enthusiasm to the field of sport.

The vast plain of green grass was marked by a course of two miles in circuit. Outside of it, near the winning post, were the long high galleries with seats for hire, and a decorated balcony for Queen Victoria. Acres were crowded with living masses. The hum of conversation, the loud oaths of the excited fancy men, the hoarse cries of hucksters, the constant peals of laughter from groups of jovial friends, the frequent strains of military music, the occasional yelp of injured dogs, the neighing of numerous horses, the rumble of infinite wagons, sounded for miles like the roar of the ocean.

The throng of foreigners and English comprised all classes. The cities and the counties—the factories, the fields, the counters, the bar, the pulpit, the press, the gaols, the palaces, the fighting rings, were represented.

Gamblers were tempting the unwary with illusive cards and little jokers. Thieves were industriously abstracting coins and watches. Showmen amused gaping crowds with Punch and Judy. Bogus American serenaders were singing Dandy Jim of Caroline. Fair country girls and high born ladies softened the coarse aspect of the scene by their presence and their charms. Lords and diplomatists mingled with the promiscuous multitude and staked large sums upon the success of favorite nags. The Queen, a small woman, with sharp features and half closed lips, attended by the Duke of Cambridge, a foreign prince, her children, and her handsome consort, gave a sort of official encouragement and national character to the day. It was a royal custom in the time of Pindar to patronize the race. The steeds of kings won prizes in the ancient circus. English sovereigns from the reign of James the First, and perhaps before, established rules, appointed courses, sanctioned laws, and entered horses to maintain the credit of the turf. Whatever tends to improve the stock, the speed and endurance of the most useful animal has been deemed worthy of the countenance of governments. The Ascot premium was an exquisitely finished silver cup, ornamented with appropriate devices and figures. More than a dozen horses appeared in the contest for it. Although evidently eager for the start, they showed no unruly restlessness, and neither champed the bit nor pranced ambitiously about. They walked with an easy swinging gait. They were thorough bred. Others for the chase, for the charge, for draught, may be alloyed with baser stock, but the racer is the patrician of his kind. His lineage is carefully recorded, and ascends higher than that of half the aristocracy. His ancestors won wagers before the House of Hanover reached the throne. His blood was unmixed before, perhaps, the Commonwealth perished with Cromwell—before the monarchy expired with Charles. Through revolutions and civil wars, in the midst of invasions and expeditions, his line has been preserved for centuries, untainted and unbroken. His derivation is traced to that country where the horse is his master's friend and fortune—where he seems to serve from choice, and to be swayed by love—where he is never degraded by labor—where he is trained for pursuit and flight on the unlimited sands, and in the wild air, of the desert—where he is compared to the eagle in swiftness, and to the storm in terror. The present stock owes its parentage to the Godolphin Arabian, to the Darley Arabian, or to the White Turk, which last was imported in the time of James.

Those on the course seemed models of breed and training. They were mostly of a chestnut color, of large size, with high withers, small ears, flat legs, long bodies, and long tails which were cut squarely off at the ends. They had no superfluous flesh, their muscles were hard and as elastic as steel, their soft hairy sides shimmered like velvet, and their large full eyes were bright as light itself. The jockeys were dressed in caps, boots and breeches, and distinguished from one another by jackets of various hues.

Amidst some confusion, the Judges take the stand, the track is cleared, the signal is given, and the whole troop leap to the exhilarating task.

They seem to fly as they recede, but turning the distant curve, their long springing motion looks like an easy gallop.

How gloriously they move along the surface, with their brilliant colored riders, and their streaming tails.

Though they started together, they soon scatter; some fall far in the rear, others droop near the lead, and only two or three show any hope in the contest. Shouts go up at intervals, when stretching forth their long necks as if they would devour the distance, they press or pass one another. The dust rises like a cloud behind them. Money is transferred from hand to hand as the chances waver. The rapid hoofs resound loudly over the field. They approach the goal for the last time. The jockeys firm upon the seat, bend over the loose reins, cheer with the voice, urge with the whip, and strike the spurs into the steaming flanks. The struggle grows critical,—the interest becomes intense,—people stand up on the benches, they gaze beneath the shade of their hands,—thousand of glasses are pointed,—exclamations are heard on all sides. The green jacket is in advance —the red is upon his quarter—the black suddenly comes up. He shows at once victorious metal—his eye balls seem ready to burst with rage—his red nostrils smoke like fires—his body appears now to kiss the ground—his legs seem now borne upon wings—the air roars as he rushes through it—he moves twenty feet at a bound—he passes the second horse—he is by the side of the foremost—he gains on him—he is on his shoulder—he is even—he is ahead—he is beyond the winning post—the flags fall—the race is won.

Amidst the wildest commotion the track is filled, the winner is surrounded—he bears himself proudly—he seems to rejoice in his triumph. His steps, his looks are watched and admired. He is regarded with a kind of reverence. He is to the course what the hero is to the field. Speed is the horse's virtue. No wonder that its exhibition is always popular, that it attracts all characters, that states foster it, that it was a pastime of antiquity, that it inspired the epic bards.

LOCH LOMOND AND LOCH KATRINE.

We glided with the gentle waters of the Leven, on whose bank Smollet was born, into Loch Lomond, the largest lake in Scotland. It is dotted with islands of much natural beauty, and much legendary interest. One contains the fierce Macgregors' graves. Another gave the war cry to the Buchanans. Another is marked by a cave, or the ruins of some grim tower or castle. Nearly all are wooded, elevated like piles of rocks, and haunted by rabbits, deer and goblins, and one, they say, by lunatics. The loch winds amongst them like streams, often narrow, always deep, and so sheltered, that the surface hardly knows a ripple or a wave. Rough, huge, and lofty, Ben Lomond and Ben Voirlich rise on opposite sides. At the water's edge you see the entrance to Rob Roy's cave, one hundred feet in depth. The main shores are red with heather-bells, or bright with streamlets, which flutter like ribbons on the distant crags.

We passed for a few miles on foot by a devious way, between tall ridges, by cot and moor, and moss, by burn and bog, till we beheld Loch Katrine below us, brilliant as a mirror. We sailed it from end to end. The channel was circuitous, the hills seemed to close up on our path and in our wake. Birch trees covered the steep slopes with their green and silver, the soaring mountain tops blazed like altars in the setting sun. The inlets fringed with grass and boughs, the pebbly beach, the varying light of sky and shores, and the dancing shadows on the waters, made

> "It so wondrous wild, the whole might seem
> The scenery of a fairy dream."

Its very solitude inspired a belief in unseen creatures. Its silence seemed like the pauses in music. The next instant some magic might transform the sylvan picture, or fill the air with the swell of mysterious voices, or the hum of elfin wings. But Scott's wizard genius has added to the charms of this delicious region. We gaze with new interest on the haunts of chivalry and love. In yonder glen the huntsman left his "matchless steed" to "Highland eagles." Beneath the branching oaks and weeping willows of that oval island, floated the shallop of fair Ellen. There is the beach, where with his minstrel harp, reclined the white-haired Allan-bane.

There by the glade, the smitten stranger lingered for the maiden's 'mute farewell.'

There is Benvenue, whence sped the fiery cross rousing from meadow, bier and altar, Clan Alpine for the battle.

Thence onward is the Goblin's cave, the Trossachs glen, Loch Achray, the mustering place of Lanrick mead—and Coilantogle ford, where guide and guest sealed in blood their courtesies and courage—

> "Then foot, and eye, and point, opposed
> In dubious strife they darkly closed."

WOMEN.

The imagination has been exhausted in describing woman. She has been compared to a fair vision, to a lovely flower, to a celestial spirit. She has been called the paragon of creatures, the personification of frailty and of fury. She has been named a belligerent biped trebly armed with tears, tongue and nails; or a suppliant being, made to prepare the meals and mend the clothes of man. But she is rather the better, if not the wiser half of human nature, and an exquisite partner

"in the ceaseless, changeless, hopeless round
Of weariness, and heartlessness, and woe, and vanity, that make up man's mortal journey."

From the first, when it was thought not good for man to be alone, and from his side, nearest the heart, was formed a helpmate meet for him—from then till now, through all the vicissitudes of ages, places and opinion, women have consummately answered the object of their original. Their kindness and their charms have been the unfailing fountain of family felicity, the secret of social attachment, refinement and progress. They have subdued the hard nature, the fierce passions, and the rude manners of mankind. They have elicited the softer feelings, the quicker sensibilities; fostered those nicer perceptions, and finer faculties, and purer sentiments, which appreciate and constitute the harmonics of the soul. Whatever is delicate in expression or thought, or gentle in spirit, or graceful in address, or amiable in intercourse; whatever soothes, consoles or cheers; stimulates the desire of excellence, invites to offices of charity, or excites the better affections, is founded in female influence or cherished by it. That influence gives rise or exercise to every elegant art—to that which ravishes the ear with the discourse of sweet sounds, or which enchants the fancy with ideas of the beautiful, with the blandishments of pleasant visions or embodied forms, or which crowd the heart with emotions of delight and love. It is she who inspires the dreams of poetry, and the pages of romance; and flings fascination over all the field of letters, and every department of taste. What story ever moved, or pleased, or persuaded, or taught—what masterpiece of imaginative composition has genius ever conceived, or moulded, or portrayed, in which she was not the source of its merit, or the means of its praise! In her sex were personified the muses, and those graces and virtues, which still wait upon her steps and bless her presence. On her was imposed the mission to watch the holy flame of Vesta, to utter the oracles of Apollo, to dictate the laws of Numa, to communicate the Sibyl's leaves to Tarquin. In every leaf of history are her living records. It is her noiseless, social prevailing influence which has created an elegant standard of approbation. She has also mingled in the struggle for literary fame, and been distinguished amongst the gifted and the learned. Her authorship has not wanted either happy style or useful purpose. She has accurately delineated the lively features of scenes, passions and lives. Her efforts have tended to meliorate; blended wholesome principle with entertainment; rarely pandered to common prejudice, or served the corruptions of the day. She has been the advocate of better things, of human advancement; holding forth inducements to consistency in morals or in faith; decking truth with flowers; making goodness to appear bold, and beautiful, and to be desired; entwining the scales of justice with the wreath of mercy; opening the door of relief to the voice of distress; speaking encouragement to the desolate; humility to the proud, and peace to those who are at strife.

We hardly find in the catalogue of writers, one of purer aspirations, who displayed livelier pictures of humanity, with more of good and less of evil, than she who sang the "Songs of Woman," of "Home," of "The Affections," of "The Hebrew Mother," and "The better Land." There was also Miss Landon who shed new interest on scriptural stories, and the gay period of tournaments, of errant knights and minstrels. And those lovely sisters who strung their harps on the banks of the Saranack, and perished just as the world caught a glimpse of the angel purity and beauty of their lives. And Hannah Moore, whose ingenious logic combatted in England the infidel sophistry of France. And Miss Burney, whose productions first gave a sound morality to fictions in prose, and enchanted the great orator and the great critic of her age. There too are the delicious odes of Sappho, to whose memory Lesbian admiration raised temples and altars. And there are the genius of Madame De Stael, and the scholarship of Lady Jane Grey.

If we regard woman's capacity for eloquence, what natural advantages of sensibility, and fluency, and fancy! What richness of metaphor, what ingenuity of persuasion does she display! Every attribute of her sex, and every quality of her nature—the sweetness of her lips, the mild radiance of her eyes, the weakness of her person, and the reserve of her deportment, infinitely aid her.

So we read of the successful pleading of the daughter of the Lydian king, which caused opposing hosts to ground their weapons, and conclude a long and bitter struggle. And of the Celtic women who saved the nation on the eve of a civil warfare. And of Hortensia, when she victoriously spoke in behalf of the Roman matrons against the tyranny of the Triumvir. And of Miss Tucker who at the Exeter Assizes, inexperienced and alone, obtained her acquital against the direction of the judge.

If we regard her efforts for the advancement of science, what grander example than that of Isabel, who aided the adventurous discovery of the new world. Or what more interesting instance of intelligent study than that of Miss Herschel, whose original observations of the heavens were acknowledged by learned associations.

Her administrative ability has been demonstrated by Semiramis, making Babylon the beauty of cities; and by Elizabeth, establishing the glory of England. Women have been also eminent in the field. There was the military maid of Orleans, as beautiful as brave, cased in the rugged gear of war, climbing foremost "the perilous edge of battle when it raged." Or witness the famous Telesilla, whose lyrics gave lustre to the city of Argos, and whose brilliant courage saved it from the desolations of a siege. Or that queen of Carsonne, who with shield and lance drove the exulting Saracens from the city gates. Or the wife of the sixth Harry, the heroine of twelve decisive battles. Or the maid of Saragossa, whose intrepidity revived the failing spirits of her countrymen, and repulsed the army of France. Or Boadicea, the Druid queen of Britain, who headed her rude soldiery against the steady legions of Rome.

But we need not enumerate instances of individual courage, when women have gone to the field in squadrons, moving with measured tread to the sound of "instrumental harmony," and fighting till the "mailed Mars did on his altar sit up to the ears in blood." Thus the Amazonians of Asia, wild as Lapland witches, left their native hills on a distant expedition to meet the army of Attica. And the famous Jane Hachette at the head of a regiment of female voltigeurs, with streaming hair and clothes, yelling and shouting as only women can yell and shout, scared the troops of Burgundy from the town of Beauvais.

Such examples exhibit the higher capabilities of the sex when emergencies call them forth. But public sentiment considers, that it is

> "Men who must be busy out of doors, must stir
> The city; yea make the great world aware
> That they are in it! for the mastery of which
> They race and wrestle."

And that women best act their part

> "When they do make their ordered houses know them."

That they are to strive by moral influence and natural graces.

In her beauty lies a source of power. It is external and therefore is an instant recommendation. It acts like incantation; reaches the roughest heart that throbs; dazzles, fascinates and gives immedicable wounds.— It has been mightier than the sword, or sceptre, or the gifts of mind. It has ruled states and heroes; foiled philosophy in the schools; won the prize from genius in the games; wrung mercy from the judge; made the tyrant gentle; the miser liberal; the bandit honest. It was beauty which controlled the policy of Athens in the splendid period of Pericles. It saved the life of Phryne, when the reasoning of Socrates failed. It five times triumphed over the hymns and pæans of Pindar, when Corinna was his rival. It drew out in prodigal profusion the treasure of the French monarch, when the starving populace begged in vain. It stayed the blow of death, when the daughter of a savage chief interceded for a stranger. It obtained protection from the robber for an outlawed English queen. It turned away the wrath of David, when it pleaded in the countenance of Abigal. It saved the scattered Jews from massacre, when Esther besought the king. It carried the poll for Fox, when the Duchess of Devonshire reached the hustings.

Yet this female beauty is as common as sight. It is peculiar to no nation, and is claimed by no class. It glows in the goddess, and in the peasant girl, and in the Indian squaw. It reigns in the parlor, in the pantry, and in the fish market. It drinks nectar on Olympus, schnapps in Holland, wine in Castile, and signs the temperance pledge in Kennett Square. It dances on the stage, prays in the church, swears on the wharf, and smokes in Matamoras. It sings like a nightingale, and screams like a peacock. It scolds on washing day, and gossips at the tea party. It reads novels, and hymn-books, and valentines. It sews, spins, scrubs, cooks, thumps on the piano, and keeps no secrets.

It is difficult to define the source of that beauty of the face which men are prone to worship. Is it in any cast of complexion? There have been beauties colorless as air, pale as cream, yellow as gold, or red like crimson, or brown as autumn leaves. "Match me" (says the bard)

> "With Spain's dark glancing daughters."

While Helen, whose charms caused strife amongst the gods, had the complexion of smoke. Is it in the glossy appearance of the hair? Venus has been represented with a head as scarlet as fire. Is it in the regularity of features? The béauties of ancient Persia were remarkable for a nose like an eagle. Is it in

> "the eyes which are the books, the academies,
> From whence doth spring the true Promethean fire?"

Homer considered that they were only beautiful as they were large, and made Juno's the size of an ox's. And the goat feeted belles of China have them no bigger than their beads.

The standard of taste varies. It requires teeth to be gilded in Japan, painted red in India, blackened in Guzurat. The skin must be as blue as the sky in Greenland, jet as ebony in Monomotapa. In Peru the nostrils are hung with heavy jewelry; and goitres ornament the necks of Alpine girls.

Beauty seems, therefore, dependent for its impression on caprice or fashion. It is, however, the element of that attraction and sympathetic desire of hearts, which the world calls love.

Love requires no teaching. It is prior to precept, independent of rule, defies calculation and description, and engrosses every faculty and feeling. It merges all other considerations into a single impulse, and sometimes turns men into poets, lunatics and corpses. It is the bond of society, which it pervades like an atmosphere; which it gilds like sunshine, and blesses like grace.

In individual instances it exhibits infinite phases, accordingly as occasion or temperament gives it trial. It is coy, tender, serious, ardent and irresistible. It is patient of mockery, difficulty, toil, danger; unchecked by injury, indifference or doubt. It overlooks the shame, fault or folly of its object; forgives, excuses, extenuates; spares when it might punish; suffers when it might avenge; still hopes against appearances; still believes against disappointments; still confides though betrayed.

> "When the soul dejected lies,
> Love can raise it to the skies.
> When in languor sleeps the heart,
> Love can wake it with his dart."

Its influence is boundless. It reaches all periods and conditions of existence. It pervades and thrills, with trembling or anticipation or ecstasy, the feeble, the youthful, the old, the homely, the humble, the pretty, and the brave. It cannot be concealed, like murder it will out. It feeds upon the damask'd cheek; speaks in the languid eye; cautious silence and muttering soliloquy betray it. The swain carves it on the trees, and pipes it on his reeds. It clings to the wanderer as he wears his far off voyage to stranger lands. It is with the soldier on the red field of battle; with the ambitious in the fierce wrestle for fortune or for power; with him who bears the sacred vessels of the altar.

It has affected languages and creeds. It is the theme of the early ballads, and of cultivated verse. It inspired the self sacrifice of Phaon's rejected mistress; the immortal sonnets of Petrarch; the letters of Eloisa and Abelard.

Love was the subject of those prize productions, which were written in gold on the walls of the holiest temple of "Araby the blest." In the palmy days of Grecian letters, when fable crowded the elements with spirits, love was made a god, naked and blind, armed with bow and quiver, and graced with little wings. That little god still doubtless lives, and waves his purple pinions, and hurls his magic arrows into infinite hearts. For love is now as it was of old, mysterious as the future, omnipotent as death, lasting as life, and universal as woman. She is its object, and ever present cause.

> "She has the shaft of eyes
> That far the shaft of war out flies."

And we may presume that the lustre of every eye, blue,

black, gray, and hazel, has had its prey, and made its conquest.

For

> "The lover very frantic,
> Sees Helen's beauty in a brow of
> Egypt."

Without the aid of mythology or calvinism, one might conclude that love is not lottery, but fate. That its silken cords are twisted, and its gilded meshes woven by the fingers of destiny herself. Lovers, like poets, are born. Accident or circumstance only exposes the latent spark, or fans it into flame. So all the tricks of the wooer and the wooed—the leer, the ogle, the sighing, the weeping and beseeching, the Christmas present, the studied flattery, "the grave protestation and the graver oath," "the dumb jewels," and the "exhausted inkhorn," "the woful ballad," the moonlight meeting,

> "On hill, on dale, forest or mead
> By paved fountain or by rushing brook, or on the beached margent of the sea;"

The billing, the pouting and the quarrel; all potions, physical or sentimental; all philters of drugs and conjurations, are but the wayward incidents of that true passion "whose course never did run smooth."

While there is so much that is praiseworthy in woman, it must not be forgotten that an occasional one has failings, delicate and pardonable to be sure, yet sufficient to keep her within the pale of humanity. Were such a one more taciturn, with less curiosity and vanity, she would be nearly perfect, almost an angel. But these foibles prove her mortal, "of the earth, earthy." She never would, she never will believe, though inspiration penned, and miracles attested it, that when she is unadorned, she is adorned the most. Tell her anything but that, and she is as credulous as a child. She will believe in dreams as sweet as any morning ever marred; in fables as wild as the vagaries of a mind overthrown. She will believe with the schoolman, that Adam and Eve talked High Dutch in paradise; with the story teller, that three wise men of Gotham, went to sea in a bowl; with Joe Nighthead, that the mummies of Egypt, with their leathern lips drank brandy cobblers; with Sam Johnson, that ghosts have a commonwealth in purgatory. She will believe the metempsychosian, who tells her the soul of Lucretia gazes from her eyes; the gipsey, who prophesies that she will marry an Earl, and never grow old; the suitor, who swears she is sweeter than honey, and fairer than Hebe. But she never will believe that the ornaments of fashion are not the "sovereignest things on earth."

But in pursuing this subject, one feels like the hunter, when as he climbs the style, he sees a notice—"All persons are forbid trespassing on these premises." Let us then go softly towards the mysterious precincts of the toilette, and with fear and trembling enter that curious arsenal, where maidenhood arms itself for the battle of love.

There hangs the list of wounded gallants; some antidotes for ennui; the last dance; the last music; the last novel. There are cosmetics by the drawer full; rouge labeled in French, made of Connecticut brickdust and warranted to blush in every climate. There is lily whiteness, in a paste composed of chalk; a row of holiday teeth; nippers to lengthen the eye lashes; oils to lubricate the hair, and tongs to undulate it. There are extracts from bugs and flowers, to sweeten the breath, and the gloves with perfume; and essences and drugs for sudden spells of fainting and hysterics. There is the mirror to tell how to place the straggling curl, and hide the naughty mole, and display the laughing dimple, and

"To look delightfully with all the might."

There is the lady's own book, complete without a teacher—showing how the waist should be boddiced; the parasol handled; the statuary attitudes; the Parisian curtsy; the prettiest toss of the head, and swing of the train. There are gems for the fingers, and gold for the neck. There are ruffles and ribbons, and laces, and fringes, and flounces, and feathers, and boards, and cords, and cotton, about which we realize the poet's solace, that "ignorance is bliss."

Yet perhaps they would themselves pardon and favor the opposite precept.

For we find now and then a woman troubled with the desire to know! What is most forbidden, she is most anxious to find out. Her curiosity rises and falls in proportion to the secrecy of the object which excites it. The sentence of prohibition recommends the trespass. She risks the dreadful penalty to taste the fair apples, from which alone she was commanded to abstain. She would not forbear, though it should turn her into salt, from looking behind her on the guilty city. She longed to raise the lid of Pandora's fearful box; and to lift the silver veil of the mysterious prophet of Khorassan. She crossed territories to see the wisest of men, and try with him the dazzling foil of wit. She was the first to inquire about *stat nominis umbra;* and the author of the papers of Boz.

She wants to know the latest stranger, and the freshest news—

"Who's dead, who's broke, who's run away?"

Who has just been married, and how they are going to live. She wonders what they are doing at her neighbor's; whether the man with the moustache is widowed or wedded, or engaged; who was at last night's party; and what will happen next. She would like to know if it is going to rain, and hopes it will not thunder.

She would like

"To know what's what, and that's as high
As metaphysic wit can fly."

All this gives employment to "That delightful engine of her thoughts"—that little speaking instrument, which sometimes aids her charms and always her ambition. So with some, loquacity becomes a habit and a nature, which no influence can control. They will suffer persecution—they will die at the stake before that small member shall cease and remain quiescent. Though public opinion, though the church command, and one rise from the dead and cry, 'silence'—yet on it goes from

"Morn till noon, from noon till dewy eve,"

and perhaps through the small hours of the drowsy night.

In vain have laws been passed against such for babbling; and common scolds been placed under the pump. They demand the widest liberty of speech; they must talk or perish. Perhaps it is this propensity which makes marriage so attractive to some, and unsatisfactory to others; which makes it

> "Such a rabble rout,
> That those who are out, would fain get in,
> And those who are in, would fain get out."

But there are, always, serious questions in the matrimonial catechism. It would require some ingenuity to calculate the cost of that institution; to enter into the statistics of marriageable conditions, the metaphysics of choice, the economy of domestic medicine, marketing and furniture. While experience is so various, who will decide; whether disparity in age, in temper, in worldly means, in social position, in external appearance, or in substantial merit, is to be regarded or despised? It is enough, perhaps, that the apostle says, without qualification, that marriage is honorable in all. The wedding brings the novelty of change, and displays to hope interesting pictures of home, fireside and domestic blessings. But there is the sober fact that disappointment cannot be cured, and repentance will not redeem. There is the vision of an occasional digression from intra-mural peace, and nightly lectures behind the curtain, where

> "The spouse with skill vibrates her eternal tongue,
> Forever most divinely in the wrong."

There is the household burthen—a half a score of infant geniuses, with as many mouths, voracious and vocal.

There is every Monday, the rush and wrangle of "the red armed washers," who riot in all the hubbub of drabs and starch, and suds, and steam, and tubs, and pots, and fire. There is the milliner's weekly charges; the butcher's weekly dues; the doctor's lengthy bill for whooping cough and measles; and perchance, the bailiff's lugubrious shadow periodically darkens the happy husband's door.

But such connubial experience perhaps chastens the spirit.

And while there have been Caudles and Xantippes, there have been others "who open the mouth with wisdom, and in whose tongue is the law of kindness." Such was the consort of the learned Budaeus, who shared his studies, revived his energies and stimulated his zeal. Others have shown unshrinking attachment in perilous emergencies, like her

> "Who in his dark prison house,
> In the terrific face of armed law,
> Yea, on the scaffold as it needs must be,
> Never did forsake him."

Others have illustrated various virtues.

We see her friendship in the beautiful intercourse of Naomi and Ruth. Her love of country, when the exiled Jewish daughters wept for Zion, and when Volumnia's prayers saved Rome. Her charity, in the gifts and the ministering hand of Dorcas. Her humility, when Mary washed the feet of Christ and wiped them with her hair. Her faith, when Damaris believed Paul on the Areopagus, teaching the Athenians the unknown God. And great was the faith of her who prayed merely for the crumbs of the master's table; and of her who deemed the hem of the Saviour's garment hallowed with healing virtue. And admirable is the conduct of those, who now, bless by their service or their means, the righteous defence of free institutions. Thus, in all circumstances, have the sex proved themselves adapted to their position, and fulfilled the great purpose of their mission.

> "Then honor to woman entwining and braiding,
> Life's garland with roses forever, unfading."

ABBOTSFORD AND MELROSE.

Scott has made these localities familiar and famous. We seem to know every crag and moor, every burn and ruin—to realize at once his descriptions, tales and histories. His imagination, like the mirror of the alchemist, makes the past return and the unreal to appear. We witness again the fairy revels, the gory feuds, the harper's lay, the wizard's spells. Here again is the ancient Rymer who wooed the Elfin queen. Here is the magician whose body casts no shadow, whose word cleft the hills and stayed the flood; into whose mighty book mortal durst not gaze. The cliffs are again ablaze with beacon fires; the glens echo with the slogan of the clans, with the tramp of troopers, and the twang of archers' bows. From the broken walls of abbeys come the toll of vesper bells, and the chaunt of beaded friars. The palmer "who has kissed the blessed tomb," wanders again from shrine to shrine, with his scallop shell and faded branch. The old castle hall resounds with pibroch and ballad, and the bold Barons feast on peacock and wild boar. The warder's challenge is shouted from the tower. The heralds post their champions and assert their cause. The dwarf, the page, the palfry with its bells, the maiden with her flowing wimple and her petted hawk, all pass before us.

But here, also, all the personal associations of the poet are revived. Beneath yon firs, by the green banks of the silver Tweed, up those devious paths, with staff and hound, he often strayed. There are the heather hills he loved so well. This was his delectable mountain, from which he glanced over Smailholme tower, Teviotdale and Ettrick shaws, and Yarrow braes, and Gala water. There is the shattered heap of Melrose, with its foliaged window and florid dome, "so sad and fair," which his fancy, like the pale moonlight, has gilded with its silver touch. Amidst the spreading grove stands Abbotsford, his Baronial hall. A quaint odd pile of tower, and battlement, and balcony—with old mottoes on the gables, old busts built in the walls, arches and carvings copied from ruins, and heraldic paintings on the windows. A piece of architecture as various, as picturesque and romantic as his genius.

Within are rare relics—from the Ganges, frow New Zealand; of the days of Alfred, of Wallace; the pistols of Claverhouse, the gun of Rob Roy, the hunting bottle of James the First, the portraits of Charles the Twelfth of Sweden, and of Cromwell; ebony chairs from George the Fourth, wall paper painted in China. The library is large. His study contains his armchair, covered with black leather, his writing desk, his canes, his hatchet, his checkered trowsers, his heavy shoes—articles more attractive than any which he gathered.

"But hush'd is the harp, the minstrel gone."

The rooms are vacant which witnessed his tall form, his cordial cheer, his keen wit, his free laugh, his fond guests, his devoted dogs.

The grounds seem dull and drear. The green trees, the blowing roses, the soft air, suggest nothing but his absence.

> "Call it not vain—they do not err
> Who say that when the poet dies,
> Mute nature mourns her worshippers,
> And celebrates his obsequies.',

LORD BROUGHAM.

The first time I saw Lord Brougham, he was engaged in hearing an appeal. He wore a black frock coat, buff waistcoat, and plaid pantaloons. His appearance resembled somewhat that of the senior Mr. C. J. Ingersoll, of Philadelphia. His features were stern, and expressive of confidence, his eyes gray, his mouth large, and he had a peculiar twitch of the muscle at the end of his nose. He was what they call fidgety. He frequently crossed his legs, folded his arms, and changed his position. He often interrupted Dr. Adams, who was arguing a marriage question, and suggested his doubts in a very amusing manner.

On another occasion, with a card of admission from Mr. Bancroft, I went to the House of Lords.

This hall is almost a hundred feet long, and half as wide, and half as high. Two rows of red morocco sofas, for the Peers, rise from an aisle in the centre towards the opposite sides. A narrow balcony above is railed in with brass, and supported by elaborately wrought corbels. The walls are wainscoted with ornamented oak. Appropriate paintings fill the lofty windows and compartments. The floor is covered with a luxurious carpet of blue and roses. The paneled roof is exquisitely carved and colored. The throne is bright with gold, crystal and velvet. The brazen candelabras fling the splendor of a hundred lights over infinite illustrations of the heraldry, the heroism and the glory of England.

The attendance was full, and the Peers, as usual, sat with their hats on. The French occupancy of Rome was to be discussed. Having reinstated the Papal government, France still occupied that capital with her troops. This excited the suspicion of other powers. Lord Brougham denounced it. His voice was not musical, but full, flexible and strong. He spoke with a fluency not usual amongst Englishmen, who generally, like Lords Palmerston and Russell, hesitate as if for a word or an idea. His manner was natural, and he "suited the action to the word." He had not the dramatic grace of Everett, whose gestures seem to follow his imagination up the shining steps of his golden climax. Nor the trembling fervor of Choate, who appeared to wrestle with the inspiring angel of his nature. Nor the persuasive style of Prentiss, as he touched those sweet notes which, like the heavenly bird's in Swedish fable, made one forget the hours. But his gesticulations were defiant, as if he dared denial —or menacing, as if he would force conviction—or derisive, as if he disdained dispute.

Sometimes he pointed with his finger; sometimes he brought both hands down in parallel lines, swaying his body forward. He was often very witty, and set the house in a roar. He was generally sarcastic and vehement. He commenced rather abruptly. He advanced a step, and elevated his arm as if about to strike a slashing blow with his fist. His voice rose to the loudest pitch, and seemed to shake the fixtures. His sentences poured forth full, round, and rapid as grape shot. His countenance, not handsome, became, as it were, grand with rage. He concentrated all eyes steadfastly upon him; stern old warriors looked as if stirred by a trumpet; beautiful women leaning over the bannister, quivered with emotion; foreigners, who did not understand the language, were excited by his earnestness; some reflected in their features every impulse of the moment, every feeling he uttered,

"Breathed his passion, echoed his scorn;"

Some seemed to shrink from him as in fear; some glowed with admiration. Every person, in one way or another, paid an unconscious tribute to the force and fascination of his eloquence. It was an effort not unworthy of one of the first characters of his time.

And however much men may call his genius eccentric, because it invades so many departments of knowledge; and his information superficial, because it is so universal; and depreciate his papers on science, his criticisms in literature, his decisions as chancellor—yet none can fairly deny his excellence in what Quintillian describes as true oratory.

"Auld Ayr, wham ne'er a town surpasses
For honest men and bonnie lasses."

The appearance of Ayr is not prepossessing. Many of its houses are of stone or clay, one story high, and roofed with straw. The river divides the town, but the streets are not clean. The ocean is at hand, but the air is not sweet. Women drive carts, push wheelbarrows, and have yellow hair. People are generally polite, talk with a broad accent, grow tall, incline to believe in ghosts and fairies, and drink hot whiskey punch after dinner.

The scenery is not grand. The hills are small, the streams narrow, and the sea view is obstructed by the island of Arran. The place is nevertheless attractive.

Near by, in a small cottage, about twelve by fifteen feet in size, an old woman sells ale, and shows the recess where, in 1759, Burns was born. His portrait on wood, and the walls, and chairs, and tables, are scribbled over with pilgrims' names.

In sight, is "Alloways auld haunted kirk," small and low, with a bell still swinging on one of the steep gables. It has no roof, a plane tree grows within it, the walls are covered with ivy, and pierced with three windows and a door.

A grave digger, quaint as Hamlet's, pointed out where the mare "Maggie stood right sair astonished," and forward, where Tam O'Shanter himself was bewildered at the boisterous frolic of the witches, the roaring storm, the blazing coffins, the bloody banquet, and auld nick, in shape of beast, blowing with might and main, the infernal music. A stone's throw off, is the narrow brig of Doon, now grass grown, over which Tam fled from the hellish legion, after he expressed his admiration for cutty sark; and whose key stone cut short her pursuit, his adventure, and Maggie's tail.

The Burns monument is near, containing his bible, and the inimitable group of Tam and souter Johnny, by Thom.

It was here, by the straying waters, by the haunted ruins, in the harvest, in the market, in the ale house, at the cottar's hearth, by glen and brae, on rock and heather, the bard wooed the muses and the lasses. His humor and pathos, his sense and genius, his sufferings and his follies, have alone given an enduring interest to the neighborhood of Ayr.

MISAPPLIED INDUSTRY.

Labor, wisely directed, is the true object of life, and the whole duty of man.

This is the spirit of the Divine ordinance—to which rest is a wholesome exception, and of which sloth is a pernicious infringement.

The motives to action are as universal as the conditions and periods, as the senses and faculties of existence. Men act from the love of business; to extinguish a rooted sorrow, or corroding care; to avoid the perils of accident or contrivance; to meet the necessities or caprices of life; to acquire political interest or lasting fame; to satisfy the cravings of avarice, of vanity, revenge, or pride; to discharge the grateful offices of charity or faith.

While every field is occupied, every effort has an influence. Nothing, indeed seems too high or mean, or difficult, or doubtful, or dangerous for human endeavor and impression. There is hardly a measure for man's industrial faculty. It creates incumbrances, or surmounts, or removes them. It achieves, or applies, or destroys results. It strengthens or despoils itself; it fulfills or ruins the purposes of life.

But it is known only by its exercise, and to be approved, it must be employed for salutary ends. The ability which has been perverted, the energies which mankind have misapplied, might have made the earth as lovely as Eden. History, then, might have been spared the recital of melancholy truths. The world would not have been such a scene of suffering and shame, nor human nature shown such examples of folly. There would not have been witnessed the alternate or combined ascendancy of delusion and discord; nor the the ceaseless oscillations of opinion, shifting the character of merit, and unfixing the standards of civil obligation and social order; nor the terrific ebullitions of public passion, overturning or shaking the organizations of force or reason, and scattering abroad corruption and disaster.

If wisdom had always guided the operations of power, its means would have been multiplied, and its results blessed. Man's condition would have been elevated, his happiness promoted; the blood of armies and the wealth of nations would not have been spent in desperate struggles in the cause of fanaticism, of rapine or revenge. Gorgeous dwellings would not have been constructed for idol deities, or vain-glorious kings. Monuments would not have been piled up to infamous or obscure names. Costly inclosures would not have been formed for whatever is brutal or trivial, in human exhibition. Garlands, pageants, and protection would not have been prepared for successful tyrants, or fortunate fools. Wild and imaginary theories would not have been pursued without regard to the analogies of nature, or the utilities of life. Learned inquiries would not have been made about phenomena which existed only in dreams; or about futile distinctions of arbitrary signs, and uncertain shadows. If folly had never ruled, vanity would have had no column, no trophies, no victims; superstition would have had no temples; ambition would have filled no thrones, established no forts, waged no wars. Neither the son of Darius, nor the son of Philip would have crossed the Hellespont; the one to return like a fugitive, the other to perish in the blaze of an eastern debauch. Athens would have saved the the blood she lavished in the engagements of the Peloponnesus. The Punic chieftain would not have accomplished a vengeful oath; and the invaders would have spared the ancient mistress of the seas. The renown of Mithridates would not have been owing to the number of cities he besieged, or dimmed by the overthrow he suffered. Marius would not have turned a parricidal hand against his country, nor repined her wandering exile amidst the desolations of Carthage. Cæsar would not have carried terror amongst the tribes of Gaul, nor passed the Rubicon, nor fallen in the capitol.

The barbarian hordes would not have swept with fire the fair fields of Italy, nor the streets of the imperial city.

The wild chief of the Tartars would not have raised a pyramid of human skulls to immortalize his infamy. The Corsican would not have channeled Europe with his camps, to grace his shoulders with the purple, and lift his family up to thrones.

England would not have turned her cannon against the feeble or the barbarous, to enlarge her possessions, and multiply her markets. The political heresy of secession would not have risen, like a fiend from the stygian vale, with bloody tongue and flaming brand, to war against the peace and progress of the great Republic.

And see what intellect has been engrossed and wasted by schools of sophistry and mystery. When the arts of magic and astrology were cultivated by a class of juglers in Chaldea; whose boasted astronomical observations proved the earth the shape of a ship, sailing in an ocean of air. When Zoroaster and his disciples taught flagrant follies, and inculcated the worship of perpetual fire in the Persian temples. When the Gymnosophists on the Ganges ranked indolence and abstinence the chief duties of life, and the chief virtues of religion. When the learning of the Egyptian and Ethiopian priesthoods was concealed in the mystery of hieroglyphical symbols, and confined to speculations on the spiritual merits of crocodiles and cows. When the Celtic race of Druids veiled their knowledge in the seclusion of caverns and groves, to sustain their mystic order, and their horrid ritual of human sacrifice.

When reverence was paid to that imposing system of Caballa in the sacred nation, founded on the oriental superstition of emanations from the Deity. When permanence was given to those divisions of the faithful—of the Sadducees on the one hand, who insisted on the identity of soul and body, and the mortality of both; and the Pharisees on the other, who swayed the Sanhedrim and the Synagogue with the traditionary corruptions of the text, and the plausible hypocrisy of forms. When the early christian fathers mingled speculative dogmas with the epistles of apostles and visions of prophets; or sanctioned absurd fictions; or the practice of allegorical interpretations, or ascetic rules and habits, thus shaking the authority, and confusing the simplicity of the truth revealed.

And see what labor was lost in those few centuries of darkness, when almost the universal mind seemed involved in sleep, so profound that it scarcely gave the slightest evidence of its powers. When the written tenets could not always be understood, or read by those ordained to teach them. When the grossest license was granted to the worst propensities; and the meanest merit disgraced the highest station. When the narrow summary of the trivium and quadrivium was the essence of scholarship; and the treasures of literature were buried in the dust and cloisters of abbeys; or burned in the flames which bigotry or barbarism kindled. When the ignorance of Bœotia, and the corruption of Corinth cursed the largest portion of the christian church.

And see what ingenuity was misapplied in that later period, when occasional lights glimmered like stars in the gray dusk of morning. When the mind showed signs of awakening consciousness, but seemed laboring under the influence of lingering dreams. When reason resumed her post, but not her office; justified her strength, but not her usefulness; and was employed in sterile logomachies about a system of scholastic subtleties. A system which started in the Lyceum of the Peripatetics, was kept alive by the zeal of the rational Mussulmans to defend the authority of the Prophet, and the absurdities of the Koran; and transmitted, at last, through devious channels, and in an altered guise, to a new order of metaphysical fanatics.

These, like the erudite devils of Milton,

> "reasoned high
> Of Providence, foreknowledge, will and fate,
> Fixed fate, free will, foreknowledge absolute,
> And found no end in wandering mazes lost."

Like the Mirror of knighthood,

> "They knew the seat of Paradise,
> Could tell on what degree it lies;
> * * * * * * *
> They could reduce all things to acts,
> And knew their nature by abstracts."

They waged fierce contests about degrees, properties and forms, the significance and construction of verbiage, the condition and quality of essences, the duration of infinity, the virtue of numbers, the impossibility of motion, the contemporaneous and separate existence of individuals and universals, the malleability of music, and the substances of angels and ideas.

Some seizing hold of irresistible difficulties of human belief, applied them, as a principle of skepticism; to assail the foundation of all knowledge. Others, enthusiastically eager to exhibit the intensity of their faith, and mistaking the true mission of the scriptures, regarded them too fondly as the only source and compendium of universal science. Others, loading the sacred writings with philosophical scholia, made a system of theology which seemed neither human nor divine. Others, rejecting the proprieties of sense and reason, devised schemes which implied their possession of supernatural virtues, and named themselves the illuminated of God. And yet all were so imbued with reverence for prescriptive names, that the dogmas of ancient sects predominated in the schools; the Stagirite was more potent than the apostle, and the sacred assemblies often listened to the ethics of Aristotle, instead of the epistles of Paul.

Thus salutary innovation was checked by those who obtained a catalogue of transcendant titles, and the tribute of posthumous honors, for corrupting language, contriving fallacies, and obscuring truth. They labored, but, like the athletes, for exhibition. They displayed ability, but accomplished no end. They disputed, they criticised, they abridged, they compiled, but they did not instruct. They produced books, but not knowledge. They invented theories, but discovered no truths. They sowed the field of intellect, but with mischievous seed. They had a harvest, but it was of thorns and thistles. No useful growth appeared, no flowers bloomed, no fruitage ripened.

Such instances of misdirected talents are only to be regarded, that they may be avoided. They who would dedicate themselves to worthy purposes, must recognize other standards, and imitate other models. They must not be seduced by the glare of false lights; nor discouraged by the failure of false efforts. Every guide is to be shunned, whose rules teach nothing but display; whose example illustrates everything but virtue; whose achievements have engendered mischief, or left no mark.

Every principle is to be discarded which narrows the circle of the sympathies; which promotes the selfish inclination of the passions; which militates against the natural evidence of the senses, or the natural suggestions of the conscience.

But that is a proper course to pursue which tends to dissipate error, to diminish the force of temptation, to increase the attractions and influence of merit, to diffuse the blessings, and enlarge the capacity of rational enjoyment.

Those labors are laudable which promise to explain some phenomena; apply, develop or improve some useful principle or agent; which supersede vicious indulgence by intellectual productions; which organize what was scattered or discordant in politics or in morals, giving to both the facilities of system, to concentrate their means and extend their advantage; which faithfully discharge the salutary requirements of public interest and responsibility; which illustrate life by consistency and benevolence.

Those characters are to be emulated who, having beneficially applied great energies, stand prominent and conspicuous—the foreground figures in the panorama of the world. They are the aristocracy of history.

Whatever merit the race can boast of, whatever advancement it has made, whatever hopes it may cherish, next to heaven, they are the source and authority of them all. Theirs is the earnest oratory which has gushed from the rostra, the tribune and the pulpit; the rapturous melody which has dropped like honey from the lips of sweetest bards; the streams of wisdom which have flowed from the closet and the grove; the revelations which have issued from the laboratory, the observatory and the cabinet; the interesting features of the past which graphic pens have delineated; the faithful representations embodied on the painter's canvas; the life-mocking creations of the sculptor; the glory which wise counsels have shed over communities and nations; the garland of honor which encircles the heroic patriot's forehead; the blessings which follow the steps of the philanthropist from hearts his alms have gladdened.

He who desires to act well his part, must observe such exemplary results; but he must do more; he must look behind them, and see how they are evolved. He must go to nature. She has her libraries, her lyceums, her academies. She has no useless volumes, no false professors. Her language is plain, her dogmas orthodox. No incongruities mar the harmony of her system; no absurdities alloy the value of her precepts. She yields her stores and attractions without reserve or limit. She directs her votaries to her works—to the universal evidence of life; to the infinite combination of materials; the diversity of forms; the mingling of colors; the diapason of sounds; the variety of relations; the re-invigorating principle of change.

She exhibits the marvelous union of flesh and spirit; their distinct spheres and characters; their separate capacities of pleasure, and pain, and usefulness; their different standards of merit and reward; their adverse and opposite inclinations; their disproportionate influence and destiny. How the one is enduring and unseen; the other transient and visible. How the one acts by contact; the other without it. How the one ranges over the past, the distant and the future; and the other is restricted to the present and the near. And how they yet co-exist, and are mutually dependent and reciprocal. How the mind secures the impressions which the sense presents; abstracts, compares, and represents them in imaginary forms and clusters. How the passions and the reason struggle, and then harmonize; control the conduct; shed lights and shadows, gay scenes and sad, over the pathway of life.

Nature points from these, from time and its relations, to her great first cause and author.

Let the student docile listen to His words. They teach what oracles could not tell, what philosophy could not prove—mortal origin and destiny. They promise what has no other source—wisdom undefiled.

That wisdom is adapted to every era and locality, and every stage of existence. But it is especially appropriate to that early period, which preceeds the drawing nigh of evil days; when the nature is pliable and plastic, and the affections fresh and warm; when the spirits briskly flow, and the blood dances in its channels; when the thoughts are unshackled by the chains of habit, and the heart is unhardened by accummulated sin; before the memory is stuffed with loathsome recollections, and the attention is deadened to impressions by the multiplicity of cares; before disappointment has chilled the ardor of hope, and injuries roused the vindictiveness of passion; before misfortune's bitter chalice has been tasted, and the frame and faculties droop with the debilities of age; before the day is far spent; before the morning dews are dried, and the bloom is wilted by the heat of noon—learn then that wisdom to which all other things shall be added. It can mould the early attributes toward good, and counteract the besetting solicitations, and easy opportunities of evil. It smooths the rough, and enlightens the dark places of life. It is a friend that sticketh closer than a brother. It avails more than human learning. It is dearer than rubies, stronger than the sword, fairer than flowers. It is lasting. But faith shall be absorbed in sight, prophecies fail, laurels wither, power decay, earth fade, death shall gather his last harvest, and "the dissolution of all things shall ripen." But the wisdom which cometh from above, shall endure in more radiant regions—the source of sweeter pleasures, and holier raptures than the eye hath seen, or the ear heard, or the heart dreamed.

He who has studied the past, the real and the pure with diligence—who has strayed "by the flowery brooks that wash the hallowed feet of Zion," has made no unworthy preparation for the eventful age we live in. An age in which peace and war alike, shall, have their victories.

Some great transitional period, some culminating point in secular history, or prophetical development seems to be at hand. Extraordinary indications; signs in the heavens; the expectations of the church, suggest such an opinion. Distrust, discontent, and impatience of restraint pervade society. There is a tendency to social and political disorganization. There is the threatened disruption of empires and republics. There is the passionate inclination for the sword—the gathering of armies and navies—the occasional roar of battle, and the steady preparation for universal war. Such opportunities, such incentives to good and evil, were never before offered to ambition.

But whoever would discharge his duty, must have a proper estimate of his powers—must exercise unflagging patience and absorbing energy—must remember that devotion to country and to freedom, are cardinal obligations—that the cause of truth must ultimately triumph—that the temple of Virtue is always the vestibule to the temple of Glory.

A TRIP IN IRELAND.

Having landed in Belfast, we passed through a fine district, mostly level, sometimes rough and rocky, through Drogheda, with its tall towers and frowning gateway; across the Boyne, once stained by battle; along the sea shore to Dublin. Here is one of the finest streets in the world, wide, straight, and lined with elegant houses. At one end is Nelson's pillar, at the other, across the Liffey, College Green.

The way was crowded—there were ragged men, barefooted women, dirty boys, servants and constables in livery, gentlemen mounted, carriages and windows filled with handsome ladies, flags flying from house tops, arches gilded with beautiful devices and brave words; and the noise of the surging throng was like the roar of a distant storm. A small woman, with a sharp, ruddy face, sat in a vehicle, bowing on both sides as she passed. It was the British Queen, leaving the city amidst the curiosity and the acclamations of the Irish.

We spent many pleasant days in this interesting capital, teeming with wit and beauty.

"A christian before baggage," said the conductor, as he cleared me a seat in the car. We passed through a valley stretching towards the horizon, vast and even as a prairie. The harvest was ripe for the sickle. The oats waved their luxuriant tops for miles. The barley, with its streaming beard, flashed like silk in the sun. The reapers were already "filling their bosoms" with the wheat, and here and there, it was heaped together like stacks of gold. The meadows, fresh with living grass, were feeding armies of cattle. The air was pure and sweet as morning. Every thing was beautiful and joyous. One felt glad and grateful, and was ready to cry out—

"Oh! Christ! it is a goodly sight to see,
What heaven hath done for this delicious land!"

But the panorama moves on, and the picture fades gradually away. The scene is changed to a dreary flat, black as pitch, as if it had been charred by a storm of fire. It is painfully sterile, without a bush or weed in view. It is one of the bog fields with its treasures of peat, the grave of forests older, as my Irish neighbor said, than creation. Trees have been taken out ten and twelve feet beneath the surface, hard and tough as metal. But the soil itself is fuel, and is cut with knives in the shape of bricks, which are piled in pyramids to dry. Huts are occasionally seen in the form of mud ovens, some with, and some without windows; with no floor but the ground, and no chimney but the door. In such places, diseased, destitute and desperate, many wretched creatures live and die. Some of them imputed their misfortune to that terrible visitation of eighteen forty-six, which (said an eye witness) lined the road sides with the carrion of the starved. A woman, coming over the rugged plain in her fluttering rags, seemed like the very genius of poverty. She had no shoes, no bonnet, and her hair streamed like a pennant; her tall figure was scarcely half clad; her voice was plaintive as misery itself, as she asked us—"A ha-penny for the love of God;" and blessed us with a beggar's prayer.

Every stopping place in the south and west was crowded by clamorous mendicants—crippled, blind, deformed and sick. There was a mother with an infant, whose face was shriveled as if by age—a man without legs, walking on his hands—a girl disfigured and disgusting as a leper. All were brown with accumulated filth, and patched with rags, various in kind and color, hanging about them loose as leaves.

It was both pitiable and picturesque, and affected the imagination and the heart. One was entertained by the diversity of tatters, features and condition; but it was impossible not to feel the conviction of want, and the necessity of alms.

Our course came at last to a still wilder country, as we approached the sea.

Hills rose up, covered with plantations of firs, or bare with rocks, or crowned with the ivied walls of old feudal castles. Here and there was an old abbey on the plain; or a "round tower" eighty feet high, distracting the learned with the mystery of its origin and purpose. We went through a little village, a few hovels were on the wayside. The children were playing in the puddles; the doors were open; and the pig walked in and out with the authority of a proprietor or partner, "switching his tail, as a gentleman switches his cane." He has the freedom of the cot, as other benefactors have the freedom of a city.

The cholera, raging violently in Cork, prevented an extended stay in that city, celebrated for its harbor and its markets,

> " And its bells of Shandon,
> That sound so grand on
> The pleasant waters
> Of the river Lee."

Kinsale is one of the old towns, with narrow streets, a Spanish ruin, and a battle field. Cork was once described as being near to it. The description is now reversed.

The first Lord Kinsale gave his name to the place. It is said that in a trial of strength, he drew the sabre of his adversary from the log, and buried his own so deep, that no one but himself could remove it.

He was then, as the King's champion, authorized to make any three demands. Accordingly he was allowed to wear his hat in the King's presence—to have a plate and stool placed for him every day at the King's table—to have in fee all the land he could, in one day, ride over on horseback. He, however, traversed only five or six miles, as some of his enemies got him intoxicated at Ballanspittle, which fixed at once, the limits of his excursion and estate.

Not far from the town, are the mansions of J. Redmond Barry and J. B. Gibbons, Esquires, whose houses, like "Marathon, look on the sea." They were most hospitable, and declared: "that during the famine, the Chester county donation of meal was the best which came to Ireland, and that it saved a thousand lives." The destitution had been frightful; there was neither food nor money; the people were terror stricken, and these provisions arrived at the very crisis of the calamity. For this timely succor, the Irish of Ballanspittle will ever gratefully remember the county of Chester.

Those gentlemen, years ago, had been extremely kind, when the good ship, Albion, was wrecked upon their coast. They showed me the scene of that disaster; and the rock from which my father, the only cabin passenger saved, was hoisted to the bank. It is a perilous place, even in fair weather; the waves wash over it; and the iron sides of the shore, bare and precipitous to a prodigious depth, make it fearful,

"And dizzy * * * to cast one's eyes so low."

SHAM SMUGGLER

The following incident which happened to Mr. B., as he arrived in London, illustrates some of the tricks of swindlers.

He was gazing about the Tower, musing on the historical crimes and sufferings, of which that London Bastile had been the scene. A person dressed like a sailor, came up, saying: "Excuse me sir, would you like to buy some real Havana segars?" Such applications had been disregarded before; but as he mentioned the word dollars, and asserted himself an American from Bangor; B., with a throb of patriotism, and an appetite in the premises, went with him. They crossed several streets, through by-ways, and a dingy court, and a sort of bar-room, into a small private chamber, furnished with a red bench and table. The establishment was the resort of the lowest order of society.

Having bought a handful of segars, he was about leaving, when the other called in a comrade with a sinister eye, rough red hair, and the complexion of a convict. This individual represented that he had lately landed from China, after a long voyage; that he had spent his funds; owed for board; and desired therefore to sell a soft white cashmere shawl, which, with other things, he had purchased in Canton for his sister. On account of his importunities, and as he would certainly refuse such a trifle, B., offered him two pounds for it. Considering that he asked fifteen, the former was astonished at the alacrity with which he sacrificed the difference. They then entered, by a crooked alley, another place which seemed like a depot, for stolen goods; where getting silver for a note B. paid him. The other then immediately wanted to sell for the same sum, a similar shawl, a dozen linen handkerchiefs, a silk vest pattern, and a gold chain wrapt in a rag. Without examining the articles; without any use for them; with a growing suspicion that the fellow was a smuggler; with some sympathy for his well acted distress, and much impatience to get away; B. paid the price, crammed them in his hat and pockets, and resolutely left. When he was ruminating in his lodgings on the fatuity with which he had been decoyed into quarters not very safe, and into a purchase of doubtful propriety; he noticed that the rag around the watch guard was stained with blood. He was confounded by the discovery—by the horrible association of blood and gold—by the predicament in which it placed him. Every circumstance which he could recall, confirmed the worst conjectures. That mean ruffian face, those vile haunts, the rich stuffs, the paltry price, the absurd story, came up like witnesses of crime. Some cruel murder must have made those fatal stains. These pretended sailors must be some obdurate villains, who had slain and plundered. These articles were the spoils of guilt. This unwitnessed purchase relieved them, and imposed on him the responsibility of possession. He felt instantly that he was burthened with all the consequences of the transaction. He alone perhaps, had the evidence of some vile deed.

It was a miserable secret. Like the Spartan's fox, it could not be exposed without shame, nor concealed without distress. Silence would make him a wilful accomplice—publication might cause him to be accused as one.

He had no friend to consult. He could not trust a stranger. A magistrate could not be informed without detaining him as a prisoner or a witness. Yet the offence must soon be discovered; the parties perhaps arrested. He would then be implicated, described, advertised as a criminal, pursued by the police.

Embarrassed by these reflections, he searched the newspapers for some clue to the mystery. For days he did not venture into the street, lest he might be recognized. He feared every ring of the bell, and every sound on the stairs.

At one time he intended to communicate the affair to the Times, but weeks might elapse without an answer. At last he inclosed the articles with an anonymous note to a bailiff, and at dusk went cautiously out to mail them. But the scheme failed, the package was too large to be admitted into the post box; and disappointed he returned to a restless pillow and to evil dreams. Nearly a week had been lost. Anxiety had preyed upon his spirits, and disturbed his health. On another evening however, after the usual hour of rest, he arranged the package under his coat, and wandered forth to throw it into some basement window or balcony. He envied as he passed numerous parties, who yet lingered, laughing and chatting beneath the bright gas and stars. Weary and nervous, searching for a spot where he could deposit the bundle unseen, he went on for squares. He had reached a building with an iron inclosure in front; and as no one was in sight, he was about to toss the package behind it. Just then a person stepped suddenly around the corner, and gazed on him carefully. He had observed the same one soon after he started out; he was manifestly a policeman in plain clothes, who had been attracted by his manner, or the distended appearance of his coat. Hurrying forward he knew not whither, through lanes and cross streets, perspiring with exercise and emotion, he came at length to an unfrequented place on the outskirts of the city. He breathed more freely, he was congratulating himself on success, rebuking himself for idle fears; when hearing steps behind, he turned, and beheld, with increased alarm, the same person.

He immediately determined to return to his lodgings. Taking a circuitous direction, he hastened along without stopping, faint and weary, for a mile or more. It was midnight; and avoiding as much as possible the regular watchmen, he chose the most dimly lighted streets. The silence was only broken by his own foot-fall, echoing loud enough, it seemed to wake the city. He was ignorant of his bearings, until he found himself before the frowning walls of Newgate prison. The grated windows and dull gray stones almost made him shudder, as they appeared to look down with a kind of ominous triumph.

Turning aside again into the first alley, he was soon crossing a deep trench, lately dug for a sewer. The distant lantern shed a dull twilight over it. Tempted by this fortunate opportunity, he was hesitating again, when the shadow of some one attracted his notice. His pursuer had stopped near the light, and cast a menacing look upon him as he passed. He followed him then directly; was always near him; sometimes behind, sometimes before him; halted when he did; walked slow and fast as he did; and eyed him with insolence. Self respect could endure no more; and B. then turned and advanced upon him with resolution and defiance. The watcher retired, believed himself mistaken and disappeared. B. got back to his room, unmolested but unsuccessful. His last adventure was dangerous indeed. Had he been seen throwing away that package, his worst fears would have been realized. It would have been impossible to have satisfied the witness of his innocence; and for that night at least, perhaps for many others, he must have endured a prison.

Though exhausted and prostrated, he retired with some satisfaction, for having escaped the consequence of this blundering excursion.

Another morning still found him in possession of the cursed purchase, which seemed to cleave to him like the fabled gift of Nessus. Defeated in all his plans, his distress noticed by his landlord, he on inquiry divulged to him at once all the facts. Having called his wife, they looked at the articles, asked the cost, and to his surprise and relief, burst out a laughing. These shawls were made in Manchester, and the price is seven shillings—these handkerchiefs are cotton—this vesting is not silk—this light chain is galvanized brass—this rag is stained on purpose.

Those men were the agents of swindling shops; they take such methods to make an impression that their articles are cheap. It seems they study human nature closely. They play upon the imagination. They invest their dealings with a degree of mystery, to excite an interest. They assume to be sailors in order to avail themselves of the attractions of that character. They trust to the natural sympathy of landsmen for those who brave the seas. They rely on the universal love of romance; on that fascination which attaches to a reckless heroism, by which the smuggler's offence is overshadowed by his courage and his perils. They elicit one's confidence by silently depending on his honor. They make him a customer by adroitly enlisting his sensibilities. Thus was he beguiled. He was yet glad to know that none had been injured but himself. That fact lifted a burthen from his conscience. It was like the cheerful daylight dispelling a dreadful dream.

PARIS.

Some years ago, while in Paris, my window fronted on the Boulevards. That street is an entertaining show. The throng pours incessantly along, exhaustless as a river, promiscuous as a world. On they move—far up, far down—all day, all night—fast and slow—crossing, turning, passing—interminable as a circle—a procession without a van, and without a rear. All classes and characters—infants and women, dotards and cripples, traders and travellers, rogues and Christians, mingled together, on foot, on horses, in vehicles—laughing, talking, dreaming; seeking pleasure, money, knowledge, mischief, fame. The policeman with blue uniform, white buttons, moustache, cocked hat, sword and the conscious air of office. Soldiers in different garbs, colored like the spirits in the play, marching in battalions, or strolling in couples, listless as children. Political aspirants, speculating on place and suffrage, on times and seasons. Legitimists, praying for the day which should crown the lineal Bourbon. Socialists, panting for the triumph of the blouses and the barricades. Orleanists, scheming to re-build the constitutional throne. Bonapartists, anticipating the restoration of the Empire. True Republicans, fearing, with good reason, that those liberty trees at the corners would bear no fruit, that "their roots would wither, and their blossoms go up as dust." There is the flower girl with her gipsey hat and olive face, singing and selling her fragrant wares.

There goes the Englishman, stout and ruddy from ale and beefsteak, with his guide book and umbrella, essential as his clothes. The American, all in black, with segar and cane—still vain of his own Republic. The German, with heavy brow and beard, perhaps a fugitive scholar from Bonn or Heidelberg. The Jew, still unfairly described as faithful to his Sabbath and to Mammon, ready to bargain with kings or thieves. The solemn Moslem, in his turban and flowing robes. The negro, with tangled hair and "trimly dressed," perhaps a colonial representative of France. The Priest, in dark gown and upturned chapeau—the sister, with her beads and silver cross—the student, in his semi-military coat—the seamstress, without a bonnet—the hackman, with a gilded band upon his hat—the porter, with a medal—the postman, with leathern sack and crimson collar—the laborer, in blue shirt—the dandy, in white vest—the mourner, in her weeds.

They are wending in all directions, on the wide pavement, beneath the arching trees, by the tall white houses, by the shop windows brilliant with jewelry and glass; by stalls filled with pictures of the Empire and Napoleon; by restaurants and cafes, where women are clerks, and both sexes feed on scientific soups, or indulge in smoke, coffee and cogniac; by the monumental gates of Saint Martin and Saint Denis, associated with foreign victories and the barricades; by the classic columns of La Madeline, designed for glory and appropriated to religion. Towards the Place Vendome, and its shaft of captured cannon, pictured with battles, and crowned with a colossal figure of the Emperor in his favorite costume; towards the Place de la Concorde, once stained with royal blood, now adorned with exotic flowers, with lanterns and fountains, and a monolith from Thebes; towards the Champs Elysees, animated with spectacles, and games, and music, and merry as a fair. To the marble arc of triumph, sculptured with the martial history of the nation; to the Champs de Mars, the scene of political festivals, and the sham-fights and reviews of armies; to the Hospital of Invalids, where the scarred veterans guard the dust of their great captain; to the National Assembly, to hear the historian of the consulate, or a greater, the historian of the Gironde. To the Bourse, within whose half a hundred Corinthian columns, blind fortune turns her delusive wheel; to the Palaces, with their sumptuous furniture and innumerable decorations of art and curiosity; to the Court, where M. Berryer enchains his listeners with rare eloquence; to the Conciergerie, whose gloomy gates closed on Marie Antoinette, and whose tocsin sounded the fatal eve of St. Bartholomew; to the Pantheon, suggested by a woman, sacred to the great, containing the tombs of Lannes, of Rousseau, of Voltaire; to Notre Dame, where the captive Pope crowned the soldier of fortune. To the Hotel de Ville, where Robespierre held his councils—where poor Louis assumed the red cap—where La Fayette presented the Duke of Orleans to the people—where Lamartine with words of inspiration exorcised the fury of the mob. To the equestrian statue of the great Henry, on the spot where templars were burned for sorcery; to the remains of the Temple, once a stronghold of crusaders, and the last prison of Louis the Sixteenth; to the Garden of Plants, enriched by Buffon, Cuvier, and others, with specimens from every department of natural history; to the metal column of July, over the site of the Bastile, and the bones of its destroyers; to La Morgue, to see the last corpse found in the street, or in the Seine; to the news-room, to read the last page of history.

JUDGE STORY.

Omnes ex omni ætate, qui in hac civitate intelligentiam juris habuerunt, si unum in locum conferantur, cum eo non sunt comparandi.—Cic.

Judge Story was of moderate height, with regular features, and an amiable expression of countenance. His forehead was broad and high, and increased by his baldness. His nose was slightly aquiline, his cheeks neither lank nor full, his mouth handsome; the little hair on his temples was of a sandy color, and his complexion of a sanguine hue. His head was compact and symmetrical. He was very active. His step was quick —he drove fast—he was always in a hurry, and yet always unaffectedly courteous. His presence inspired cheerfulness, and you could see gratification in every face, the moment he appeared. He was extremely fascinating to young men. He met them with a sweet smile and a kind voice. He grasped both their hands, with a warm pressure. Sometimes he would lay his arm on one's shoulder.

He was an incomparable law lecturer; all the variety of an intellectual entertainment he shed over that dry subject. He scarcely got seated before he commenced; and without notes, continued in a delightful, flowing manner, retaining universal attention till he closed.

His discourse teemed with humorous anecdotes, and literature. When something recalled to his mind an incident at the the bar, or a peculiarity of a great character, he would describe a scene or a speech, or repeat a sentence or a gesture, with enthusiasm. Sometimes becoming excited by the course of his thoughts, he grew theatrical, gesticulated with vehemence, partly rose from his seat, and spoke with wonderful rapidity and eloquence.

Devoted to the law, he was fond of light reading.

He referred to himself (which he seldom did) as having written verses, when he was young, but no poetry. He excused himself once for not being punctual, by saying; that he was unconsciously delayed by an interesting article in Blackwood. He told, with some proper pride, that, when in the Massachusetts Legislature, he was instrumental in increasing the salary of Chief Justice Parsons, whose judicial ability he could hardly sufficiently praise.

And he assumed reasonable credit for having done his duty, in deciding the first cause before him, against the influence of the government, which placed him at thirty-three years of age, on the Supreme Bench of the United States.

One day, when interrupted in his lecture by the passing of a volunteer company, with a band of music, he good humoredly said from Cicero—"*Silent leges inter arma.*" He frequently referred, with admiration, to the gigantic mind of Jeremiah Mason; of whom Webster said, dig as deep as you will, Jerry will dig deeper. He lamented the death, at an early age, of Hugh Legare, of South Carolina, whom he considered a ripe scholar, and the best civil lawyer at the American bar.

He remarked that a lawyer's first duty was to his God, the next to the law, the next to his client.

He said Luther Martin distinguished himself in the trial of Judge Chase, before the Senate. That when he came to reply to John Randolph, a splendid orator, but no lawyer, and who was chief manager of the impeachment for the House of Representatives; he utterly scattered and demolished all his positions. And so the lawyers, succeeded then just as Mr. Law and others did in the trial of Hastings. Judge Story said he studied law under Chief Justice Sewall, who told him that whenever he had a cause of importance, he commenced his investigations with Blackstone.

He said of William Pinckney, of Maryland; that he was very attentive to dress, generally carried a switch, wore tights and gloves, and came in that style into Court. That he appeared anxious to avoid the reputation of having studied; and on the evening before he had a cause to argue, generally contrived to attend, for a while, some entertainment; and afterwards devoted the rest of the night to his preparation. But yet to a friend who expostulated with him on his injurious attention to business, he replied; that " it was only by great labor he had won his position at the Bar—that it was dearer to him than life, and; "By G–d! he would die to maintain it."

Pinckney was but a boy when Judge Chase took him into his office; and when he was sent by Washington as Commissioner to England, he attended the Courts of Westminster for six years. On one occasion, in company, and not knowing Greek, he was quite confounded by an argument respecting a passage in Euripides. From that time he studied the classics. He had a wonderful memory, and mastered every subject he touched. He was learned in every branch of the law. He had a guttural voice, but the most beautiful and peculiarly expressive diction.

He was an honest lawyer—to the court, the law and his client. Chief Justice Marshall remarked to him (Story) that Pinckney was the most powerful reasoner he ever met.

One day Judge Story said of Judge Chase, that he was a large, broad, six foot man, for all the world like Dr. Johnson; gruff and impatient of long arguments. A lawyer once said to him, "I am going to make five points." "Good G—d!" exclaimed Judge Chase, "five points!" After hearing them, he said, "they are good for nothing," and would allow only two of them to be discussed. Another time, he dismissed all the points, and decided in favor of the counsel on a ground he had not noticed. Once Luther Martin convinced him of an error. He had a far reaching perception, and saw conclusions at a glance. At Washington, when I (Judge Story) was a young man, I boarded with him. On leaving, he took hold of my hands and said: "I would that I had seen more of you, or had never seen you," and burst into tears.

Another time, Judge Story described Chief Justice Parsons, of Massachusetts, as one of the greatest judges; he was at home in the sciences; had a famous wit, which enlightened, but never scorched; and was fond of ladies' company, who admired him, though he was by no means handsome. Like Chief Justice Marshall, who was the closest reasoner I (Judge Story) ever met; he loved novels, and found as much pleasure in the law as in a romance, and as much pleasure in a romance as in the law.

Another day, Judge Story speaking of the Girard case, in which he had delivered the judgment of the Court, said: "Mr. H. Binney was perfect master of the subject. He had been, perhaps, studying it for a year; had long before given an opinion in favor of the validity of the will. He came to the task incited, no doubt, by the desire of sustaining his former conclusion; and by the fact of having to contend against one of the first minds of the age—in the highest tribunal of the land." Mr. Webster represented the heirs. The Judge, in illustration of Mr. Binney's thoroughness of preparation, said he himself had discovered certain reports of cases very pertinent to the gist of the cause; and which he thought no one but himself had noticed, and took them to his room to look over. Mr. Binney, however, inquired of the Librarian for the book, who directed him to Judge Story, as most likely to have any stray volume. The reading of these reports took Mr. Webster by surprise. Both Mr. Binney and Mr. Webster, he said, made great speeches, worthy of Westminster Hall in her best days. But Mr. Binney delivered the law argument; which answered all the requirements of criticism, satisfied the highest legal taste, and influenced the result. While part of it, which lasted for about a half of an hour, was so finished and beautiful, so subdued and powerful, that the Judges, after he concluded it, looked at one another and smiled. He added, that it must have certainly been written and committed to memory.

Judge Story, at another time, alluded to Alexander Hamilton as an extraordinary man; one of the great intellects in history; capable of resolving the most important questions, and happily qualified for the inauguration of a new government. When General Washington had some scruples as to the constitutionality of a United States Bank, he applied to Hamilton to remove them. The President then lived in Philadelphia, and his Secretary went to the house of William Lewis, an eminent lawyer in the height of his fame. Having stated the object of his visit, they stepped out to Mr. Lewis' garden, and in a peripatetic consultation, enduring the afternoon, weighed the question in all its possible relations. Hamilton then returned home, asked his wife for a cup of strong coffee, as he intended to sit up all night. The next morning, he handed the President a written argument, sustaining the constitutionality of the Bank, which was satisfactory. There has been, continued the Judge, nothing since said or written on that subject; on the bench, or at the bar, in Congress, or in newspapers, which is not contained in that narcotic and nocturnal paper of Alexander Hamilton.

The Judge once spoke of the elder John Adams as a lawyer; who, when Vice President, was appealed to for his opinion on the force of the "common law" in this country. He at once declared that it existed of necessity. That as far as consistent with our condition, it was operative of course, for it was assumed as the basis of our legislation.

On another occasion the Judge referred to the Dartmouth College case, which excited very general interest. Mr. Webster, said he, who wields the club of Hercules entwined with flowers; appeared then for the first time in the Supreme Court. His fame preceded him. William Wirt was his opponent, "*arcades ambo.*" The Court room was filled with the aristocracy of office, talent, beauty and gallantry, such as the Capital of the country could furnish—soldiers who had been in battle—Ambassadors from Europe—members of the Cabinet—members of Congress—and elegant women who crowded around the sitting Judges, and almost allured them from their dignity and their chairs. When Mr. Webster rose, he began in a low tone, and said; that he appeared in behalf of a poor Indian School; to repay the debt of gratitude imposed upon his youth; and to use in defence of his *Alma Mater* the arms she gave him. He then went on, gradually increasing in energy and eloquence; his voice growing clearer and deeper; his gestures becoming more animated; his face more expressive; his language more passionate. The veins upon his forehead swelled like cords; his eyes flashed fire; his whole body seemed possessed by his awakened genius; his spirit pervaded the hall like a superior influence; and he carried away the Judges, the Bar and the crowd; left nearly every eye in tears; while one military man blubbered right out. Mr. Wirt had attempted to take notes, but his susceptibilities were overcome; he repeatedly threw the pen down, and at last in despair, lifting up his head towards the speaker; resigned himself to the irresistible spell. When he came to reply; he confessed that he had some points in the cause, some plan of discourse, but that the gentleman's eloquence had thrown him into confusion. After this handsome tribute he made a glorious argument himself.

SWITZERLAND.

Basle, with intricate streets and pleasant fountains, and ancient gateways, looks down upon the Rhine. The inhabitants once had scriptural texts over their doors; were compelled to dress in black on Sunday; and had their clocks one hour in advance of all others. They speak French and German, live in houses with garrets of four and five stories high; show the autograph of Luther, the dwelling of Erasmus, and the pictures of Holbein.

Our route lay hence along the river, by pear and apple orchards, and fields of sprouting grain—by timbered mountains, colored like tapestry, with autumn leaves. Thence by plains, where men drove huge cows, hitched by ropes, to wooden harrows, and to ploughs with wheels. By vine clad slopes, animated with the labors of the vintage. Women, in bare arms and red hoods, gathered the grapes in deep baskets, strapped, like knapsacks, to their shoulders; and wagons, laden with the purple harvest, were hauled, amidst songs and shouting, to the wine press. Farther on, the landscape embraced new features. There was a cultivated valley— three winding rivers pouring their waters into one—the town of Brugg, with its lofty walls and conical towers— the Abbey of Kœnigsfeld, with its enclosure, like a city—the ruined castle of the first of the Habsburgs—

and girding them all, high as the clouds, far around as half the horizon, crowned with ice, and glittering like a silver zone in the sunset, rose the eternal Alps. We watched the enkindling scene till it disappeared with the day.

The next afternoon we were climbing, amongst vagrant cows and courteous citizens, the steep, crooked, narrow streets of Zurich. The eaves of the tall houses overhang like porticos. Spires abound, painted and sharp as spears. Promenades extend along the ancient ramparts. The lake, the river, and the mountains gratify the eye. Zwingle, the hero and scholar, began here the Reformation. Here Lavater, the physiognomist, and the two Gessners, the naturalist and the poet, were born. The arsenal is full of curious weapons of old Swiss wars. It contains a cross-bow, of wood and iron, with which, they say, Tell shot the apple from the head of his son.

Traveling through drifting clouds, an elevation of two thousand feet, cultivated to its summit, we descended, by roadside crosses of wood and iron, to Lucerne. It lies between the heights of the Righi and Pilatus; and on the shores of that lake, which is forever associated with the progress of liberty, and the epic history of the heroic Swiss. There are numerous bridges in the town, spanning turbulent rapids, and adorned with paintings.

In the suburbs, is a monument to the Swiss defenders of the Tuilleries, designed by Thorwaldsen. Carved out of the solid rock, with a limpid pool of water beneath it, lies a colossal lion; which, fatally pierced by a spear, holds, with dying strength, the Bourbon shield in its paws. It wears an expression of pain and courage, of fidelity to duty, and resignation to fate—passionate, spiritual, and natural. One instantly feels, how beautifully genius has wrought this metaphor in stone; and how fitly, the king of the forest illustrates human virtue.

A two days' journey brought us to Berne. It is seated on a lofty platform of rock, surrounded at the base by the river Aar, more than one hundred feet below it. Snow covered mountains are in the distance, and fruitful valleys near. The houses are built of stone; and massive arcades shelter the sidewalks. The women, with wide sleeves, flapping like wings, and white linen vests and colored skirts, seem as though their toilet was unfinished.

Berne seems as fond of bears as Rome was of geese. The image is on its coins, and on its shield. Its effigies, in stone, mount the barriers, and crown the fountains. A clock in the street, sets in motion, when it strikes, a company of bears. Some on horseback, furnished with the mail, spurs and lance of cavaliers; and some on their hind legs, bearing swords and flags, march around in military order. In a sort of cellar, on the edge of the town, at any time of day, may be seen the animal himself; corpulent and indolent, sitting on his tail, and holding up his arms like a beggar, to boys and strangers, for apple cores and chestnuts. The city, however, liberally supports the beast, from which it derives its name, and whose bloodshed consecrated its foundations.

We passed Freyburg, with its feudal watch towers, and its wonderful gorge, crossed by the longest and the highest bridges in the world. Then through Lausanne and its shaded walks, where Gibbon completed his history.

We next reached Geneva, renowned for watches, reformers, refugees and poets. Thither went John Knox, fleeing from Britain. There rested John Calvin, driven from Italy. It has been the resort of royalists, from France; regicides, from London; and plain rogues from all places. It was the birth place of Rousseau. Near it, Byron wrote some of his cantos. Near it, Voltaire passed his latter days. It is built in a charming valley, partially encompassed with a double line of fortifications; forming a promenade, from which you look up to the loftiest mountain, and down on one of the loveliest lakes in Europe. The place seems in everything but location, a French town. You find French waiters in the hotels. You read French newspapers in the cafes. You see French signs over the shops. You hear French all through the streets. You pay your bill in French coins. You ride away in a French diligence. You can hardly distinguish a native from a Frenchman.

But the Swiss have a national character, and in general are honest, polite and penurious. And as their country is rugged and mountainous, circumscribed in extent, with small towns and few factories; without seaports, or navigable rivers, or railroads; they can never be a great people. But as they are industrious, they cannot be poor. And as they are brave, they will always be free.

JOE.

Joe is a character. Nature has done something for him, and promises more. That he will be taller, heavier, and older, if he lives, may be confidently asserted. We cannot as easily aver that he will be scientific, poetical, or wealthy.

He is not a prodigy for a boy of fourteen, like Pascal. He may not become as admirable as Crichton; or as handsome as Absalom. He does not read or write out of his vernacular; and uses the gift of speech with apparent reluctance. It is unlikely that he will ever move masses by his tongue, or be as eloquent as Belial, or Ulysess. He will not supply the lost works of Livy, or restore the lost arts.

His mathematical information is limited. He is satisfied that a hoop forms a circle, and that the globe is round, like a marble. He will never calculate the inclination of an asymptote, nor invent a theorem, like Maclaurin's. He has no tendency to astronomy. He seldom looks up, unless he is under a fruit tree. He would not have regarded the falling apple in the same point of view as Newton. He has not inhaled that divine afflatus, which inspires spondees and dactyls; though his drowsy disposition gives him the dreamy look of some of the poets.

The colossal fortunes which industry and economy have raised; the transient but irresistible fascination of political eclat; the hazardous but brilliant game of soldier, may never be connected with his name.

He ignores the maxim about the early bird getting the worm. Most probably he will never run for office. He is not without pluck or patriotism, but his sympathies are *statu quo ante bellum.*

That activity which never tires, and is aptly compared to the ceaseless motions in nature; that energy which overleaps difficulties, crushes opposition, and wrenches success from defeat and despair; he cannot be said to illustrate.

His phrenological features display a well balanced mind, such as Everett, calls genius. His impulses are not violent, nor is he liable to explosions of wrath, surprise or mirth. He is not facetious, nor profound, nor plausible, nor presuming.

He is peculiarly and pre-eminently slow. A quality which is, however, not without merit or friends. The precession of the equinoxes is slow. Justice is slow, and moves in leaden shoes. A slow punishment gives a chance for repentance. "Be slow to anger," says the scripture. A slow match often saves life. A slow foot, like that of the tortoise, sometimes wins a race. A slow soldier, like Fabius, often throws a foe off his guard. A slow coach has charms for nervous women; and a slow note, for a poor man. A slow cure promises most health. A slow growth, like the persimmon's, conduces to vigor. A slow process of making money is apt to be successful. A slow dog, like the beagle, is likely to worry down the game. A slow fire, like a burning knot, is certain to last. A slow rain penetrates the earth. A slow eater gets fat. A slow life is mostly a long one. And slow people are said to be sure. They are not in a hurry to go or stop. They do not break anything in order to see a balloon or a circus. They are content "to wait for the wagon," or the millenium. They are rarely alarmed; they seldom get hurt; they are not choked; they are not cheated. They do not get lost; they do not abscond. They are serious, they are doubters; sometimes skeptics, never enthusiasts. They are often melancholy, never frantic; though apt to make others so, who depend on their motions.

Therefore nothing is more intolerable than a slow cook to the hungry; or a slow priest to the bride; or a slow express with returns, to the politician. Nor in any such capacity ought Joe ever to be employed.

Indeed, it is difficult to say when, he will be the right person in the right place. He has hardly sufficient momentum to be mischievous or meritorious. He has not zeal enough for a parson; and yet too much humility for the Bar. He is not positive enough for the Bench; he is not systematic enough for a physician, and he is too conservative for a quack.

His local attachment must prevent him from going much abroad. His reserve would, besides, make him rather insipid, as a traveling companion. In a two day's excursion, a horse-trough, like one at home, elicited the only remark he made.

His habits are sedentary. He would be eminent as a tailor, if it were not for the laborious motion of the arms; as an errand boy, if it were not for the constant draught upon the legs; as a nurse, if vigilance were unnecessary; and a good lad generally, if he had nothing to do.

His innocent face evinces no emotion, and excites none. He does not seem to be thinking of anything that ever occurred; or expecting that anything would happen again.

He fully illustrates that expression of repose which is so characteristic of Egyptian art. If the ancient mythology prevailed, he might be employed as a model for that immovable deity, which was planted on boundary lines, and called the god Terminus. For this purpose, had he not been so slow in being born, he would, two thousand years ago, have been useful in the world.

THE SIMPLON PASS OVER THE ALPS.

In a diligence we passed over meadows, where shepherd girls, in razeed hats and roundabouts, watched browsing cattle; through villages with streets of mire, and houses roofed by overjutting rocks, the abodes of Cretins and goitred women; amongst ravines filled with firs, and the wrecks of avalanches, till we struck the Simplon.

This road was the work of Napoleon. It required six years for its construction, and often the labor of thirty thousand men. Its length is nearly fifty miles; it pierces the granite mountain in a dozen places; spans gorges with more than five hundred bridges; and with a width of twenty-five feet, and a grade of an inch to the foot, ascends more than a mile above the sea.

We entered the pass before dawn. There was no moon, but the outline of things was dimly shown by the glittering constellations. There was no noise, but the occasional splash of water, and the creaking wheels. There was no traveler but myself; and I walked with slow and easy steps, up this solitude, so infinite and wild.

Great masses in front appeared to obstruct the way. Great gulfs, abrupt, and wide, and invisibly deep, yawned around. Vast shadows loomed from the rugged steps, vague as monsters. Shapeless heaps rose high and distant as the stars, which seemed to crown them. The whole might resemble the anarchy of nature—as if Hercules in his burning rage; or Milton's angels in their war, had strewed here the fragments of unseated woods and "upturned mountains."

Day broke at length, and the sun flashed from point to point, and lighted up the grandeur of the scene. Heights, depths and distances were disclosed. Rocks, huge as hills, were poised like missiles. Cliffs, like pyramids or towers, were roofed with snow, or pinnacled with ice. Trees, old and tall, swung from the sides of fearful chasms. Torrents rushed overhead or underfoot, thundering in their fall, and flinging up their spray in rainbows. Dark tunnels, long galleries, lofty arches, and huts of refuge were passed, and the summit gained. All there was barren and cold as winter. The daisies had disappeared, the grasses failed, the firs and birches took no root. Glaciers, and granite, and desolation reigned around.

The descent was hence by a narrow defile, called the gorge of Gondo, whose perpendicular sides reach up a thousand feet above the road. We traversed this winding avenue, cut through solid stone, a two hours journey, to its end.

It opened into a plain, where miles of level land were beautifully green; where vines were trailed over countless arbours; and slopes were decked with pretty villas; and gardens glowed with fruit and flowers; where the air was full of life and song, and the sky bright as pearl. This was Italy.

A RIDE ON THE PRAIRIES.

Years ago, when railroads were scarce in the great west, I crossed the muddy Mississippi, from St. Louis, and started in a Troy built stage, on a journey through Illinois. I was the only passenger; and as the driver ostentatiously gathered up the "ribbons," and gave his whip the dexterous flourish of his craft, and the four horses sprang forward in a gallop, and the coach danced on its leathern springs, I seemed confidentially vain of my importance.

On we went, the dust rolled away like smoke behind us; houses and fields in constant succession disappeared; long miles were made; and the day was well nigh spent, when we halted at an Inn, whose sign was a picture of our own conveyance.

The next morning, we were again on the road, through acres of corn, which prevailed over the wide land; sometimes through a wooden village built on cord sticks, with a small office, used by turns for church, court and school. Our arrival in such a place, heralded by the rattle of hoofs and wheels, and a blast from the stage horn, brought out the chief citizens. There was the man who had been cast, the justice of the peace, the Methodist brother, and those unofficial loafers, who claim to be the people.

Sometimes, for great distances, there were no signs of cultivation; no roof of shelter, no growth of grain, no fenced ground, no single tree was to be seen. The vast level expanded in all directions to the horizon; sublime in its uniformity, its solitude, and silence. The long grass rippled like water in the breeze; brilliant with gay flowers, and that delicious green, which only virgin soils and prairie suns produce.

Again we went by clumps of wood, thick with bushes, whither the deer retreat from the heat and the flies. The prairie chickens, in flocks, flushed suddenly before us, or sailed lazily over the road. The rattlesnake, now and then, trailed swiftly through the dust, or coiled up in the way, struck defiantly, and vainly at the wheels.

No person met us on the route; but some cattle stood, like pictures, against the sky, as we approached the "Traveler's rest." We remained a while at this isolated tavern to shoot game. It was built of frame, painted red, and leaned far out of plumb. The barroom was decorated with wagon gear and chains; with two long flint lock guns, and two huge powder horns; with several whiskey jugs and tins; with doors which had neither bolts nor locks. The "Sucker" landlord smiled inquisitively, and soon asked: "whar I came from." The children wondered at my wristbands, and said they were "mighty white." The wife prepared a supper more wholesome than fashionable.

Having slept on the floor, and gunned around the house, and eaten a prairie hen, I left, next day, in the stage.

At night fall, when we stopped for water, an unknown person took a seat beside me. Being able only to see that his figure was tall, I indulged in some fancies about brigands. But weary of loneliness and silence, his society was a relief, and we chatted for a time pleasantly together. His misuse of sounding words, however, made an impression that he was silly or eccentric.

Soon the sky grew darker with gathering clouds; the stars became obscured; and the breeze augmented to a gale. Having been silent for a while, my companion suddenly said—"Stranger did you ever know the king of the Spanish dominions?—he is a great man—I correspond with him—he is my brother—do you know him?" Raising his voice, he proceeded:—"He has soldiers, and spirits, and devils—he is the man in the moon!" Startled and alarmed at thus finding myself alone, at such a time and place, with a crazy man, I involuntarily seized the door, and nervously answered, no. "Not know him;" he said more loudly—"Not know him—how I pity you—you shall know him—I'll take you to him—I'll introduce you—we'll go to night—hurrah to night!" In the midst of his cries, the storm increased—the blast redoubled its fury—the rain beat upon us like a flood. Then, with an abrupt lunge, we were borne forward with new speed; the horses were running away—the coach rocked from side to side, as if it would overturn. We were thrown against one another, backward and forwards, while on we dashed—down in the gullies—over the sluices—up the hillocks—now clattering across a rickety bridge—on into thick darkness, made more fearful by the gleam of lightings, and the crash of thunder bolts.

While amidst this confusion ; arose the frantic yells of the lunatic, to aggravate the dread and the danger. It seemed, indeed, as if the spirits he spoke of, were present, and his promise of our destination would be fulfilled. A thousand thoughts flew through the mind, of the past, the distant, of home, and kin, and sin, and death. Nothing but a catastrophe seemed likely to stop us. All at once; we were hurled violently, head foremost, to the front of the stage, and stunned, for a time, by the shock. A few minutes afterwards, we crawled out to find that we had lost a wheel, and were lodged in a marsh.

As I recovered, and stood in the drenching rain, the lunatic ran off with wild speed, shouting more wildly— "Hurrah—Spanish dominions—dominions—hurrah," till his voice, broken and diminished, in the distance, "grew fainter and then ceased."

A cottage happened to be near, and the storm lulling, the hospitable squatter, with a lantern, assisted us to restore the wheel, and lash it fast by a hickory withe. The driver then, to an inquiry about our late passenger, said ; that he had become deranged for the loss of his brother on the coast of Spain ; and that usually quiet, he had been roused to fury by the tempest.

We then went softly on our way, with all possible caution, without delaying the United States mail, for the erratic correspondent of the King of the Spanish dominions.

FROM THE ALPS TO PISA.

Leaving the Alps, we saw peasant girls with large throats, red bordered skirts, red turbans and dark surtouts; carrying leaves along the road; or picking them amongst the perilous rocks, like those who gathered samphire on the cliffs of Dover.

We entered the luxurious vallies which had so often allured invaders; passed villages, diversified with the painted walls of houses; the yellow legs of lazaroni, the flow of dirty waters, and women with olive cheeks and raven curls. We followed the sinuous shores of Lake Maggiore, whose islands, small or populous, resembled floating cities, or ships of flowers. We reached Milan, where the officers of customs looked narrowly amongst our baggage for pamphlets and pistols, and a gang of porters, acquired by degrees, our smaller coins.

Milan was prosperous when Rome declined; was wasted by rivals and barbarians; was famous for its steel, and gave a name to Milliners. The streets are paved with a double line of flat stones; over which carriages roll as smoothly as on a floor. Prints and paintings are tacked upon dead walls. Cauldrons of large chestnuts are roasting over charcoal fires, and huckster men ladle out a handful for a "sous." Beggars are sitting contentedly at the corners; rattling money boxes, as the dice players do for luck. Women are passing with black embroidered veils on their heads, in lieu of bonnets. Balconies are hanging from the windows. An ancient colonnade stands desolate in the streets. Tall bell towers are near the churches.

The Duomo is considered the most beautiful of Cathedrals. It is all marble, once entirely white, now somewhat tinged with the yellow hue of time. It is nearly five hundred feet in length; and more than three hundred and fifty from the pavement to the apex. The walls are relieved with buttresses, richly wrought, and Roman windows, and painted glass, and niches filled with figures. Pinnacles rise on every side—each surmounted by a statue. Above them all, the spire ascends with winding steps, and sculptured balusters; like a stairway to the clouds. On its very summit shines an effigy of the Madonna.

The interior of the edifice is also imposing. The elegant doors open on a floor of tri-colored mosaic. Rows of colossal columns eighty feet in height, support the fretted arches of the roof. Splendid monuments to saints and cardinals, and handsome altars are by the walls. Large pictures are along the corridors. Pulpits of bronze, with symbolic images, are near the choir; and in a golden shrine, arrayed in gorgeous robes, lies the shriveled mummy of San Carlo.

From Milan, our road led over a flat country; dotted with poplars, oaks and willows; by men in knee-breeches, and women with wooden heels; by white castles, and poor towns; over bridges of boats, where at night each drowsy passenger in the diligence was roused to pay his river fare; across the battle fields of Hannibal and Napoleon; down the mountain side to Genoa.

This city is seated on a crescent shore. The Appenines behind it are beautiful with vines and villas; its spires are numerous; its shops and palaces and churches are rich in gold and marble. All the streets but one are narrow; all the women wear white veils; and it has been called the city of Kings.

Hence a steamer landed us amidst the cries of boatmen and clouds of dust, on the wide flag pavements of Leghorn, which has given a name to hats.

The traveler is impressed here with the division of labor, which is so well adapted to diminish his resources. One porter hands the baggage to another; a third unloads, and a fourth carries it in to the hotel. Neither the driver nor waiter is allowed to interfere, although all the six must be paid.

A rail car bore us hence to Pisa. The leaning tower is circular, of white marble, with eight colonnades around it, one above the other. It is fifty feet in diameter, and one hundred and eighty feet high. It has stood six hundred years, leaning thirteen feet from the perpendicular. The inclination was caused by a yielding soil. It was counterbalanced, by varying the length of the columns, during its construction, and afterwards, by the bells. The largest bell weighs twelve thousand pounds; and is so hung as to keep the centre of gravity within the base.

From every position; from the street; from the top; at a distance, or near, the tower appears as if it was just going to fall. To one on the summit, it seems sinking down; but he is at once attracted by the interesting and extensive view around him. Below is the Cathedral, with the long horizontal lines, and elevated platform of a Grecian temple; a monument of pious gratitude for victory over the infidels. Near by, is the "Holy Field" inclosed, and covered with soil from Calvary; decorated with frescoes and sarcophagi. And there is the city and the winding river—the meadows with herds of cattle, white as the Cretan bull—villages on the mountain sides—and the sails of gallant vessels flashing on the distant sea.

THE DOG BOZ.

On the morning after the great Macaulay was lowered amongst the illustrious bones of Westminster, the best of dogs was found stark and senseless on the sleeted snow. Old Boz is dead; like Hiawatha, he has gone

> "To the regions of the home wind,
> * * * * *
> To the kingdom of Ponemah."

Dogs, like Indians, look perchance beyond this vale of tears to a paradise of game. The theory has been suggested by men of science, like Peter H. Browne, and by men of the world, like Samuel Weller. So we read of one's ghost, which haunted Peel castle, and deprived of speech whoever addressed it. If their treatment here has not corresponded with their conduct, it is reasonable to expect for them a compensating future.

They were the first animals subdued, and their usefulness has been most various. They have been devoted to the security, the amusement, and luxury of men. Some ancients and some moderns have deemed their flesh delicious food. Hippocrates compared it to pork. The Chinaman prefers it to veal. Dog's blood was once considered an antidote for poison. His hide has been used for slippers, and his hair for beds and robes. His instinct taught us our resort to emetics.

His habits adapt themselves to all phases of society. He hunts with the savage, and the sportsman; through the forest and the prairie. He watches the flocks, while the shepherd studies the stars—and the house of the burgher, while he dreams on his couch. He drags the rude sledge of the Esquimaux over the ocean of ice; and the truck wagon of the Boor along the highways of Holland. He invades the ambush of the wild beast and the assassin. He goes with the conscript over the perilous "ridges of battle."

He displays qualities such as men delight to boast of. He has had more applause than the clown, for his tricks in the circus. He has tracked, with the keenness of a sheriff, stolen goods and felons, through crowds, and darkness, and for weeks—torn the money from the pocket and the shoes—led a friend to the hidden corpse—sprang at the murderer's throat. He attended the wounded with the same charity as the heroine of Scutari. He guided the blind beggar after alms. He gathered food for the starving—saved the helpless from the precipice, the flood and the fire. He served with equal fidelity the powerful and the poor—nor forgot his master abroad—nor forsook him in the prison—nor at the scaffold—nor at the tomb.

He recognized Telemachus, long absent,

"And fawning at his feet confessed his joy."

Homer again makes his faithfulness excite the tears of Ulysses; and Southey, the grief of Rhoderick; and Cowper compares his love to religion. He watched by the sick bed of Peter Bold. He mourned over the headless body of Mary, Queen of Scots. He wandered over the field of Dresden, seeking the slain Moreau. He followed alone the pauper's hearse, as they

"Rattled his bones over the stones."

He threw himself on the funeral pile of royal Lysimachus. He perished of grief and despair at the grave of Jason.

But all the associations of the species are not agreeable. He is wild and ferocious on the flats of Congo. He snarls all day and night in the Eastern cities. To quarrel is his privilege.

"Let dogs delight
To bark and bite,"

is one of the earliest lessons. The Mosaic figure over the "*cave canem,*" at Pompeii, is but a symbol of anger. The rage of Hecuba changed her into a dog. He is a beast and, therefore, sensual. He is liable to madness, and hence to be suspected. He is carnivorous, and may be cruel. He is servile, and may be deceitful. His voice, though a hint to rascals, and once sweet as music to the tired and plundered Syntax, is a foe to repose. He prowls amongst garbage, and does not always smell like a thousand flowers.

His name was sometimes given to the Furies. It represented the spirit of war and havoc. It has been a term of scorn. His service was ignominious. His price was unclean, and not fit for the altar. He lapped up the blood of Ahab; ate the flesh of Jezebel, and devoured the Christians in the Roman circus. Job, in bitterness, only preferred him to his enemy. The preacher, in charity, only preferred him to a dead lion.

Moses abhorred him, when he made him silent against Israel—and the Philistine, when he railed at the weapons of David—Hazael, when he scouted at the crimes predicted by the prophet—and the inhabitants of Sygaros, who would not allow him to approach their abodes.

He was compared to whatever was greedy, dumb, uncircumcised, incorrigible, or worked evil. He was compared to those without the pale of grace. Before him, the holy things were not to be cast. To him, the children's bread was not to be given. He returned to the filth he rejected. He licked the sores of Lazarus. Æschylus illustrated, by his moan, the sleeping harpies. Dean Swift likened to him the baseness of Titus Oates. The mythologist personified horror in the triple-headed Cerberus, who kept the gates of Pluto—and Byron, inconstancy, in his own dog at the gates of Newstead. His vileness suggested Curran's sarcasm on Lord Clare; and Shylock's taunt—

"Is it possible a cur can lend three thousand ducats;"

and occasioned the bitten courtier to exclaim, "God bless your Majesty, but not your dogs."

A bankrupt, according to the proverb, has gone to the dogs. It is said of successful rascals, that every dog must have his day. The crowd is most desperate and dangerous, when through the town they cry, mad dog. The invalid, when most forlorn, complains of being sick as a dog. The loafer is always as tired as a dog. The worst type of constable was Dogberry. The coarsest of philosophers were called dogs, or Cynics. The most oppressive part of the year are the dog days.

The meanest of dead languages is dog Latin. The vilest poetry is doggerel. The most worthless article is dog cheap. A crafty fellow is a sly dog. A low fellow is a dirty dog. A selfish, heartless, unscrupulous fellow is usually reproached with being his relation.

Thus the prejudice of centuries, and the customs of communities have disparaged the brute. His body has been crucified along the Roman ways, and burnt upon the heathen altars. He has been made the target of satires and of stones. They have tortured and worried him, for experiment and mischief. Poisoned him, to test drugs and gases—exhibited his misery for amusement—made it no larceny to steal him—set a reward upon his head—shot him as a nuisance—chained him like a culprit—cropped his ears for fashion—shortened his tail for a joke.

Thus subject to untoward fortune, he has yet not been without favor and protection. Mohammedans place food and water for him in the streets. The Japanese have a hospital for him in sickness, and make his destruction a capital offence. Dr. Norman professed to cure his diseases, at Fox court, London. An annual exhibition is held in England to improve his breed. And a sort of poor house has been founded for him there, when he is astray or starving.

Men treat him with more familiarity than all other animals. Alciphron invited both his friend and his dog to a feast. The dog of Alcibiades divided with his master, the attention of Athens. Evander had a pair of dogs by his side, when he went to meet Æneas. The famous Blue Beard was always attended by his pack. The Queen Henrietta risked her life to save her lap dog. The poet said of the merry Charles, that—

> "His very dog, at council board,
> Sits grave and wise as any lord."

Selwyn, the wit, and Walpole, the gossip, spoke of their spaniels, as admiringly as they did of the fair Miss Gunnings. John Randolph kept his two hounds with him on the floor of Congress. Willis fondled one at Idlewild, who had smelt the "open sea." Voiture speaks of ladies, "whose eyes weep for dogs, and murder men." A spinster is said to have feared that her whiffet would get sick from biting her guest. Mrs. Barbauld calls the mastiff

> "A safe companion, and almost a friend."

Most persons are fond of a similar pet, who goes with them in their walks, their toils, their sports; excites their attachment; enlists their care, and whose death recalls his peculiar virtues.

Boz was neither

> "Mongrel, puppy, whelp, nor hound,
> Nor cur of low degree."

He was called after the popular pen of Dickens, and born a setter. A breed more ancient than the poet Surry, to whom some attribute their training. But to tell his genealogy would be as difficult, as

> "To trace the Kilmansegg pedigree,
> To the very root of the family tree."

His line runs back to the heroic age of hunters, when wants were simple and law was scarce; when there were no lectures on the "social forces," and no actions of trespass in the Common Pleas.

His ancestors may have set quails in the thickets of

Thessaly, at the "to-ho" of Diana—or with mistaken instinct, pursued and devoured imprudent Actæon—or coursed along the banks of rivers with mighty Nimrod—or yelped in the pack of Cyrus who, says Xenophon, was devoted to the chase—or caught for Cleopatra the wild boars, with which she feasted Anthony—or followed the bugles of St. Eustace—or led the hunt of mediæval Bishops over the sedges of Hainault, and the hills of Jura.

He had all the marks of gentle blood. He had the fine fluctuating ears which the Carthaginian Bard described. His form was handsome—his limbs and features, perfect and harmonious. His color was of mingled white and brown, like the leaves and frost of autumn. His hair was flowing, and soft as the fleece of Cashmere—as any the caterpillar spins, or Jacquard's loom can weave. His eyes were lustrous and sad, like a thoughtful woman's, or a poet's. He smiled, not like Cassius, but with a subdued and persuasive air; and he almost wept with human tears.

His attitudes and movements were so full of grace and and nature, that he must have allured Europa from the spell of Taurus; presented a tempting model to the artists—attracted the pencil of Landseer, and the gentle muse of Somerville.

He was docile and intelligent. He knew his duty and discharged it better than many bipeds. He could not like the spaniel of the Medicean noble, wait at table, and pour out wine—nor did he, like the one which haunted the Paris Opera, love music; though he howled a sorry second to the church bell. Nor like the one which ran with London engines, did he enjoy the excitement of a house on fire. He had not the piety which the Ettrick Shepherd claimed for his, who sat in the pew alone and kept awake. Nor the wit of Walter Scott's, who understood his stories. Nor the faculty of speech like the cur of Leibnitz; nor the gift of prophecy like Achilles' horse, or Balaam's ass.

He was swift. But he would not have equaled those who won the Pentland hills for Sir W. St. Clair, from King Robert Bruce. Merkin would have beat him who went a mile in four minutes; and Thanet's hound who ran one hundred and twenty miles in a day; and those

"Two dogs of black St. Hubert's breed,
Unmatched for courage, breath and speed."

His smell was keen. Vermin never escaped his sense and seldom his jaws. He swallowed his captives with the voracity of Cyclops. He reveled in the open field, and in the marsh. He winded from bush to tussuc, with untiring zeal, and unerring instinct to the cover, where the birds nestled, or the rabbit squat. He stopped in full gallop, and rigid as marble,

"Pointed with his instructive nose, upon
The trembling prey."

The crack of the gun gave scope to his boisterous joy. He was content with the honor without the profit of victory. He was social. He kissed the horse in harness, and played with pups and children, with all the foolishness of age.

He was not selfish, like the dog in the manger. Nor mischievous, like the smuggler's, who aided his fraud; or the boot-black's who brushed his muddy tail on strangers' feet. He was modest as worth is. He never entered the house; was patient of neglect; dainty in diet; tolerant of injury; grateful for caresses. Yet amongst his fellows, he was like Wolsey—

> "Lofty and sour to those that loved him not,
> But, to those dogs that sought him, sweet as summer."

He was a Northerner; fearless but not savage; and bit when he barked. With a prejudice for freedom, he was loyal to restraint. But he did not like the cur in the fable, or the minion of party, deem the muzzle or chain an object of pride.

He was a representative character, and might have been a subject for the essays of Emerson. He was true to his mission, and Carlyle might have placed him in his Pantheon of heroes. He was conservative, and like Burn's, Luath and Cæsar, who,

> "When up they got and shook their lugs,
> Rejoiced they were na men but dogs."

He was faithful. Politicians might dodge, friends betray, women change; but,

> "He was true as the northern star."

He was not idle. In the dark and daylight hours, he went his rounds like some ancient warder, questioning all comers—following the suspicious—scowling at vagrants—fighting the thieves, like the Bagman's dog in Ingoldsby; until he fell at last, a victim to his vigilance and courage. This last act of Boz evinced particular merit.

> "Nothing in his life so became him,
> As the leaving it."

It recalled the daring of those ancient dogs, who fought in regiments for the people of Colophon. Of those who defended the chattels of the routed Cimbri.

Of that one in the arena, who defeated the elephant to amuse the sanguinary taste of Alexander. Of that one, which in the reign of the eighth Louis, on the trial by duel, (fit ordeal for dogs,) conquered the Chevalier Macaire. And of that one, which fell fighting at the feet, and for the life of Cælius, the senator.

Boz's death was in its kind, as glorious as any in the Iliad. Martyrdoms like his, have made men's names immortal. Patriots bleed for their country, in the hope of posthumous honor, saints burn for their religion for the sake of heaven. Boz made the fatal struggle, perhaps unconscious of the future; reckless of advantage; to save from larceny half a ton of coal, whose use he never knew, and never could enjoy.

So died he; who had whatever traits could enhance the value of his kind. Nature had been liberal to him. With keen instincts and vigorous powers, he had skill and prudence, from education and experience.

> "His life was gentle, and the elements so mixed in him,
> That all the world could stand up and say,
> This was a dog."

No marble shaft, to be sure, may be placed upon his ashes, such as a Welsh Prince reared over his grey hound, Gelert. But we may say, he adds another, to those who have given consideration to his race. He was one of those, who have made dogs the object of eulogy, monuments and worship—the subject of a treatise by Caius—of poetry by Nemesianus—of painting by Protogenes—of sculpture by Miron—of history by Pliny—of anecdotes by Ælian—of fables by Æsop—of miracles by Julius Obsequens.

Such merits as his have made dogs everywhere the emblems of fidelity—the legal attendants of gentlemen in times of chivalry—fixed their effigy over the tomb of Diogenes, and at the feet of Silence—installed them as Kings in the interior of Africa—consecrated them as Gods in Egypt—and given their name to islands, to rivers, to oracles, to seasons, to cities, and to stars.

ROME.

After much annoyance from delays, charges and passports; from the police, porters, boatmen, and beggars, who would have disturbed the composure of a stoic; having bribed two of the posterity of the Cæsars, who sat for the receipt of customs, we entered Rome, saying; with the Numidian King, as he left it; "*this city is to be sold.*" It was dark, the lamps were few and flickering; no loiterers were in the streets; no revelers were abroad; the sons of Belial went not forth; it was as silent as it seemed forsaken; solemn as solitude.

Daylight, rest, and an Italian breakfast, of cake and coffee, fitted us to wander amongst its labyrinthine thoroughfares, and promiscuous population. We went along the Corso; famous for the sports of the carnival, the races of the horses, the war of sugar plums, the fantastic masks, and more fantastic tricks.

There are churches with pillared fronts, and gilded roofs, and illustrated walls; with chapels, rich as offering of pilgrim and penitent could make them—with shrines of priests, and popes, costly as thrones; and mitred skeletons, in silk and silver—with hangings of gold and crimson—with holy images, endowed with miraculous powers—with relics consecrated by age, accident or tradition; secured in iron closets, before which tapers perpetually burn—with nails which pierced the Saviour's hands; the lance which was thrust into his side; the sponge which was filled with vinegar; portion of the cross on which he hung; his vestment, which had no seam; the purple robe, and prickles from the crown of thorns; the virgin's veil, and Joseph's staff, and Peter's hair, and the tooth of Paul.

There are shop windows, filled with pictures in oil, ink, bronze, stone and shell; cameos and medallions; minature ruins; temples reduced to mantel ornaments; triumphal arches of the size of models; monumental columns, as long as candles; sarcophagi small enough for fairies; chariots which crickets might sit in and drive; beads of pearl and bone, strung on hemp or gold; precious stones in rings and bracelets; canes in bundles, like fasces or faggots; mosaics perfect as paintings and brilliant as jewels; rusty coins found or fabricated, and for sale as antique; lamps which may have lighted Cataline or Garibaldi; vases from Etrurian ruins, or modern potteries. Such things make up the commerce of the Eternal city.

Branching off, and picking our way through the filth, cautiously as cats, and holding up our skirts, like women; breathing an air which was not fresh, and smelling odors which were not sweet; we passed curves, and corners, and alleys, which seemed like sewers; vast palaces with grated windows, strong as prisons, where decayed Italian nobles lived; old arcades, incrusted with ordure, and alive with vermin and vagabonds; crowds of children, who had never been washed; an infinite variety of cripples, in distress; mountaineers clad in skins and canvas, picturesque as poetry could wish, playing their shrill pipes, such perhaps as Virgil heard, when he sang their pastoral amours.

We climbed the Pincian hill, now, as of old, the resort of wealth and fashion; and alive with whips, and canes, and feet, and wheels. The Sabine hills were white with snow. Roses were blooming in the palace yards. The winter of forty-nine was the most rigorous there for twenty years. The termagant hucksters in their stalls, and the multitudinous beggars on their beats, were seen warming over their earthen urns, filled with hot coals and ashes, the only Italian stoves; crying, in the meanwhile, their misfortunes, and their merchandise.

We stood upon the capital tower; whence the eye sweeping over the circuit of a few miles, could read the eventful history of the Empire, and its thousand years duration. The old piles of brick and marble, the single columns which, here and there, still stand like time's own sentinels; the soil which bore such monuments, and yet bears such ruins, are more eloquent than tongues or books. They are witnesses of a nation's power and refinement, errors and disasters; of a people, grand in genius, imperfect in ethics, foolish in faith; whose policy was war; whose justice was victory; whose virtue was courage; whose religion was romance.

There are fragments of temples, dedicated to ideal creations, to passions, and to chance.

There, fire was kept in perpetual flame; and there, augurs watched for omens. There, triumphal arcs still span the ways, and commemorate the desolation of towns and provinces. There, vast walls inclose the arena, in which brutal combats were displayed, and chariots raced, and christians were torn by beasts. There, are the very pavements of those great roads, over which passed all the imperial pomp and power. There, are the dreary dungeons, where kings and conspirators—Jugurtha and Cethegus were starved and strangled; and where they say Paul and Peter baptized their jailers, from that miraculous spring, which still bubbles from the floor.

Stupendous acqueducts stretch across the Campagna, with infinite arches, over which the water flowed to the ancient fountains. The great sewer, through which a loaded wain can pass, still drains, as it did two thousand years ago, the offal of the city. Outside the walls, amongst dilapidated tombs, a grand sepulchral castle frowns over Metella's grave. The waters of Juturna, clear as air, flow where the twin gods, with welcome tidings from the shores of lake Regillus, refreshed their foaming steeds and vanished. The yellow Tiber winds amongst the old foundations, washing the foot of Aventine; and over the last buttress of that bridge, where Cocles, with his single valor, kept the day against Porsenna's army.

There is Adrain's mole, built for the Emperor's ashes —once the castle of the Barons, and the prison of Beatrice Cenci, whose mournful loveliness, Guido's pencil has preserved. The Egerian grotto, mantled with dripping fern, recalls the beautiful story of the enamored goddess, and her mortal lover. Other remains of better days, and nobler men are seen at every turn. They have been built over modern dwellings; they lie loose along the sidewalks; hang feebly together; lean against later walls; and are overgrown with laurel, as if nature were wreathing them a garland.

There are fields of fragments. Shafts, capitals and cornices are strewn about beneath the feet of traveler, tradesman, and beast. Buffalos, introduced from the east, by Lorenzo, the magnificent of Florence, feed in the Forum. Oranges hang, like Hesperian apples, from the steep Tarpeian rock, whence aspiring Manlius was hurled. Cabbages are growing over half the palaces of the Cæsars. On the arches of Nero's golden house; once adorned with a thousand columns, with halls of pearl and gold, and refreshed with artificial gales— troops of cattle browse on garlic. Horses are groomed in the mansion of Pilate. Two hundred and sixty different plants bloom on the walls of the Colosseum. The baths of Diocletian, in which poets recited, and philosophers discussed, are stored with hay. Indulgence is written over the entrance to the Pantheon, the ancient temple to all the gods. The columns of the Emperors are crowned with effigies of saints. A rope walk stretches through the Basilica of Constantine. The mausoleum of Augustus is a modern circus. The gardens of Sallust are over grown with reeds. Vines are trailed over the accursed field, in which the fallen Vestals were interred alive.

There is no longer the glory and awe of empire. Fasces and games, Muses and legions, and people have been displaced. A new Rome has risen on the seven hills. With a wiser worship, but of little secular influence, the present capital is among the last, as the old, was the first of sovereignties. And though without trade, or army; its traditions, its remains, its masterpieces of the arts; and its christian temples, worthy of ancient enterprise, still make it the Eternal city.

There, on the site of Nero's circus, where the martyrs perished, as if springing from their blood, rises St. Peters. It is constructed on a scale becoming the capital of christendom; from such resources as a power deemed to hold the keys of heaven could command; by the labor of more than three hundred years. It was designed by the ablest artists; who were stimulated by ambition and devotion, to build for posterity, and eternity, a house for the Deity, which should contain the pilgrim population of the world. Its dome, soaring gracefully towards the firmament; is seen for scores of miles, from the mountains, and the shores. Its lofty colonnades, in front, crowned with two hundred and eighty statues, sweep around an area, in which an army can manœvure.

Its elegant symmetry conceals its extent. The columns of the facade, though colossal; and the pillars within, though large as chapels, seem of ordinary size. The figures of the cherubs, apparently so small, are huge as giants. The letters on the walls are legible, though long as spears. Study its details. Go around its inside limits—it is a walk of half a mile. Survey its vast variegated floor—it is measured by acres. Behold its bright ceiling, spreading above like a canopy of gold—it is higher than the forest trees. Stand near the high altar, and the Apostle's tomb—the centre of the loftiest arch is nearly four hundred feet overhead.

These distances and proportions are as harmonious as they are immense; as beautiful in part, as sublime in combination. One is no less charmed by the decorations; the eternal pictures in mosaic, and the finished groups in marble, than astonished at the magnitude of this structure—the grandest ever raised to God, or man, or idol.

Close at hand is the Vatican, with aisles, saloons and chambers; itself a city, populous with paintings and statues. There is the Apollo, beaming with supernatural beauty—love and light, and victory, deified in stone!

There is the Laocoon, with pity and horror disfiguring the same face;—torture and affection racking the same bosom;—father and sons in one peril, and in one passion;—despairing and dying, in the same monstrous folds.

There is the Saviour transfigured, faultless and first of pictures; and the Sistine chapel, adorned with the last judgment of mankind, by the pencil of Buonarotti.

A VISIT TO THE POPE.

Driven by the revolution from Rome, Pope Pius, the Ninth, sought protection and hospitality beneath the flag of Naples. And though the Republic of Garibaldi had been overturned by the Republic of Cavaignac; and his successor kept twenty thousand soldiers in the imperial city to maintain the pontifical rule—yet his Holiness, in the early part of 1850, was still domiciled at the palace of Portici.

There, not far from the buried theatre of Herculaneum; near the most magnificent bay in the world; and at the base of burning Vesuvius, he held his royal court. Sometimes he might be met in the highway, with his confidential cardinal, in a splendid coach; accompanied by outriders, and troops of soldiers, enjoying the winter air.

Having a letter from Dr. Cullen, now Primate of Ireland, to Monseigneur De Medici, the Pope's Chamberlain, I went to see him. Passing through two sets of guards, up a wide stairway, and along a dreary corridor, I was shown into a kind of office, where, in black priestly robes, were M. de Medici, and his secretaries. He received me with much kindness. When about to leave, he gave me, unsolicited, a note, of which the following is a translation :—

ROYAL PALACE OF PORTICI, Jan. 22, 1850.

The undersigned, Chamberlain to his Holiness, advises Sig. Everhart, of America, that his Holiness will give him an audience on Wednesday, the 23d inst., at 10½ A. M.

The Chamberlain to his Holiness, DE MEDICI.

Concluding to avail myself of the opportunity; and inquiring of him what costume would be appropriate, he, good humoredly, said: "Wear the best black dress suit you have, a white cravat, and no gloves."

On the appointed day, in a very unostentatious two horse hack, I returned to the Palace. Arrived at the gates, I was conducted, by an official, past the sentinels, and up the steps to a small waiting room. While a sort of military looking gentleman, with a sword, was asking about my impressions of Italy; Mons. De Medici, in purple robes, and his secretary in black silk, entered; and greeted me politely, but did not shake hands. I accompanied the Chamberlain through a large room, hung with red damask drapery, where several officers, in various uniforms, were standing before an old fashioned, open, wood fire-place. We passed on through a similar room, which was entirely vacant.

The Chamberlain then advanced into a smaller chamber, not more than ten or twelve feet square, whose walls were lined with yellow satin. Presently, he took me by the hand, and presented me, by mentioning my name and country; and retired. I was then left alone with the Pope. He was very plainly attired in a long gown of white cloth, and a scull cap, and seated at a writing table. As I approached him, bowing ceremoniously three times, he inclined towards me with a smile. His figure was full, tending to corpulency, but did not seem to be tall. He had a beautiful face, full of intelligence, and almost womanly in its expression of mildness. It was not furrowed by time, nor saddened by misfortune.

He spoke fluently, in French; his voice was gentle, his manner cheerful. He inquired about the health of Dr. Cullen, what countries I had visited, and which I preferred; the object of my travels; how far I should extend them; and if I were alone. I merely responded. He said the prosperous condition of the Church in America was of great consolation to him in his affliction. The interview having occupied about ten minutes; he handed me a souvenir, as he termed it. It was a small red case containing a medal, with his own effigy on one side, and the Virgin's on the other; around which was written, *lœtitiœ nostrœ causa.* He then bowed, as a signal for leaving, and keeping my face towards him, I retired as formally as I entered.

NAPLES.

In the winter of 1850 I was in Naples. Part of the time a blazing fire of olive sticks was necessary. Yet many trees were then green with leaves; flowers were blooming; the limes hung ripe and yellow; and hundreds of indigenous plants shed beauty and fragrance along the pleasant promenades. The scenery is remarkable. The circling hills, the clear heaven, the fertile earth, the boundless sea, the burning mountain, have made the seat of Naples famous from immemorial time. Its origin is lost in fable. Before Rome rose or Troy fell, Parthenope, the ancient city, looked upon this lovely bay.

The neighboring soil, so often rocked by earthquakes, and still smouldering with hidden fires, is strewed with the wrecks of classic fanes and villas. There were the haunts of the Sibyls and Cimmerians, of Circe and the Syrens. There were the Elysian fields, and Tartarus; the Stygian lake, and the "infernal" rivers. There the ancient gallants had every recreation for their summer hours—luxurious baths, gymnastic games, and festal shows, and Grecian art—delicious fishes, rich Falernian wine, and oysters from the Lucrine lake. There are boiling fountains; old tunnels, quarried through hills of rock; grottos, extending through darkness and water, none knows wither. Fields, sprinkled with alum and sulphur, which echo to the tread like vaults, or quiver with the roar of internal wind or fire. Caverns, emitting mephitic gases which give dogs convulsions. Hills, which have risen, and shores which have appeared, since the crusades. Lakes, over which no bird can fly; and Vesuvius with its white crown of smoke, and in the evenings, magnificent with flames, and red hot stones, and streams of burning lava.

The citizens of Naples live in a single story of large houses, whose entrance door admits a carriage. Hotels embrace only one floor. Barons and laborers occupy different flats, under the same roof; and shops are in the basement of palaces. Coral and lava ornaments, olives and oil are staples of trade. Food and clothing are cheap, though the nominal prices are extravagant. Gold is scarce, because the Jews, they say, melt it down for trinkets. Servants wear cocked hats and swords.

Begging is not peculiar to the poor, or the maimed. The man who sells you boots, the idler who directs your way, the sister from the convent, who goes veiled; as well as the waiter in the cafe, and the driver of the cab, ask you for a present. Lazaroni, unclean and lazy, lie, like snakes or negroes, on the sunny sides of streets, redolent of garlic. The wives of fishers sit knitting nets outside of the doors. Vagabonds are seen searching one another's heads with a fidelity they exhibit in no other pursuit.

The donkeys are as small as dogs, and carry every imaginable commodity—barrels, dry goods, manure, stones, wood, vegetables, furniture and haystacks. They are often without halters, but always with cruppers; and the driver, when he rides on the load, uses the tail for a bridle.

The Galesso, a vehicle with two high wheels, is drawn by one horse; whose gears, and a weathercock over the saddle, glitter with brass nails. The shafts are raised nearly a foot above the horse's back. It has a seat for two persons, but it carries a mob. The capuchin in his cowl, the priest in black robe, women in red shawls and wooden shoes, porters and hawkers of nuts and fruits, and others, nearly a score, pay a penny a-piece; and hang to the springs, the seat, the stirrups, and the axle, as it rushes headlong through the streets.

The San Carlos opera house is unequaled for size. On the King's birth night, it was bright with gold and candles. The King, a large young man, with a dull, unpleasant countenance, wore a military coat, and bowed distrustfully to the applause which greeted him. His queen and his mother were present; and their hair, their arms, and their busts blazed with diamonds. The audience were in full dress. White cravats and gloves, military feathers and epaulettes, lace and flowers, represented all the aristocracies of profession, rank and beauty; and the rarest music of orchestra and actors, charmed away the hours.

One day an officer's funeral passed the Hotel. The corpse, in uniform and uncovered, was borne on mens' shoulders. It was escorted by two priests in black, and several monks completely masked in white, except the eyes; one of whom held up the cross. A procession, with religious banners, followed, all bearing torches in their hands, and chanting as they marched.

VESUVIUS AND POMPEII.

From Resina, a small village, we started on horseback for the top of Vesuvius. There were then evident signs of an imminent eruption. With a fellow hanging to each pony's tail; passing through groups of children and mendicants; by vines and mulberries; round curves and over stones; racing and shouting, we reached the hermitage. The air was pleasant, the view vast and splendid; the wine sweet, and piously recommended as "the tears of Christ."

Passing hence over waves of lava, which seemed to have frozen as they heaved; we gained the base of a declivity, which no beast could climb. We dismounted, and up the long slippery steep; over pumice rocks; ankle deep in ashes; leaning on sticks; clutching at loose cinders; sliping over patches of snow; amidst the importunities of beggars, guides and hucksters, we toiled; perspired, and stopped. Refreshed with rest and lunch; after many falls and bruises; red in the face; panting and exhausted, we stood on the old crater.

It extended around like a plain, the surface was broken by small elevations, and deep glowing fissures. Having ascended higher, we glanced down into the huge volcanic furnace. This crater was vast in its circuit, high above the sea, indefinitely deep. The blaze, the roar, the missiles, and the quivering crust were appalling.

Explosions broke forth with the noise of a thousand guns. The whole mountain trembled. Sulphurous smoke issued out in clouds. Flames of red and blue surged against the sloping sides. The molten lava heaved up and overflowed, threatening the vineyards and villages below. Vollies of stones shot up like rockets, and came rattling back, burning as they fell. One person was struck in the face; another one on the hand; and that night, another was fatally injured. Far below us were seen the shores so often desolated by former eruptions.

We descended, and visited the theatre of Herculaneum, beneath the surface of the ground; gloomy but well preserved. We wandered through Pompeii, along the lava paved streets; across which a man could leap, and which still show the ruts of chariot wheels. The houses are generally of brick, and small; some with mosaic floors, with baths, and courts, and fountains, and painted walls. The Forum abounds with temples and columns, in various stages of decay. The theatres with stone seats, with entrances, and aisles seem almost uninjured.

But all was silent and empty. For eighteen hundred years these buildings have had no occupants; these sidewalks have been untrodden; this town has had no hum of voices, and no sound of busy life. No idle crowds go greeting through the market. No devotees climb the steps of marble fanes. No fires consume upon the altars. No sentinel, "helmed and tall," stands by the gateway. No combat stains the arena. The clatter of hoofs, the voice of eloquence, the song of joy, the wail of woe, the strife of trade, the pomp of festivals, have disappeared. Orator and augur, athlete and author, toga and stola, Lares and Penates, pageant and people have passed away. Snakes and foxes have their dens in this once pleasant city of the Classic Empire.

In the museum at Naples, are collected some of the relics of the buried towns. The sculpture which adorned their porticos. Pictured vases and articles in stone, and the precious metals, which furnished their parlors. Bottles in which they preserved their tears. The urns which held their dust. The silver mirrors of their toilettes. Papyrus on which they wrote. Gold rings and bracelets of the women. Necklaces of their nobles. A chariot of iron and leather. Their bronze lamps and oil. The metal spoons, and plate of their table. The wine and bread of which they ate and drank.

These have been taken from the ruins caused by the first eruption of the mountain, in A. D. 79. Previously, all the neighboring slopes and shores were remarkable for their culture and population. Virgil, in the Georgics, speaks of the fitness of Vesuvius for olives and vines. Strabo describes it in the same way, except the summit, which was barren. Martial celebrates it as the haunt of Bacchus, and where temples stood to Venus, and to Hercules. Tacitus also tells how its beauty was marred by the ravages of volcanic fire. Pliny alludes to the numerous towns and villas that were overwhelmed, by the eruption which he witnessed.

In a letter to Tacitus, he says; that a curious cloud of smoke, in the shape of a pine tree, rose over the mountain. That his uncle hastened, with the fleet under his command, to rescue the people, who were flying terror stricken, in all directions. That great black hot rocks rolled down to the water, and showers of burning ashes fell upon the vessels. That having landed at Stabiae, they were obliged to abandon the falling houses, and resort to the fields; with pillows on their heads, to protect them from the pelting stones. That returning to the coast, the violence of the waves prevented their embarkation. That a sulphurous vapour prevailed, which they avoided by lying on their faces, with wet napkins to their mouths. That his uncle rising, fell down suffocated. That three or four days passed in darkness, with no light but the occasional flames from the volcano, and the moving torches of distracted people.

THE ESCURIAL.

This mass of masonry is not far from Madrid, and represents a convent, sepulchre, and palace. It was designed for the honor of a saint; on whose day a victory was won; and according to the plan of a gridiron, on which he died a martyr. It was built by the first architect, under the most potent Prince, and in the palmiest time of Spain.

It is a huge pile of dark gray granite like the hills behind it; with plain rectangular walls unusually thick; pierced with little prison windows; and covers an area nearly equal to the base of the largest pyramid. It has four square towers, tapering into slender spires; an oblong addition to one side, representing the feet and handle of the model; three stone belfries rising from the centre; and two rows of Doric columns over the front entrance. Its extent, height, and sombre hue make it an imposing feature in the landscape.

In the interior are numerous courts, with fountains, and statues, and alleys paved, or sanded. Grand stairways and corridors, wide enough for coaches to pass, are arched over, and adorned with pictures, in fresco and on canvas. The chambers of the monks are plain and small. The saloons of the monarch are floored with costly wood and marble, and lined with tapestry and satin. The vaults vie with those of Thebes, in splendor, but not in size; precious stones flash light from the walls; and elaborate urns contain the jeweled sculls of Kings. Jasper columns, lofty domes, and tesselated pavements adorn the chapel. Few worshipers are seen; occasionally, a woman wearing a mantilla veil, kneels before the virgin. The Priests slip along in soft sandals to perform the morning mass.

The loneliness is oppressive. The Monks have passed away, and Royalty returns no more. The long cloisters hardly yield a sound, except the footfall of the stranger. The shady pebbled walks are overgrown; and fragrant plants waste their sweetness, like the desert flowers. Behind are barren mountains; before, are barren plains, and all around are signs of decay. Capacious houses are near; many were never finished; some are in ruins; most are deserted. Weeds cling upon the walls; bats and lizards peer from the crevices; storks beat their wings upon the chimines; lean black pigs root along the alleys; goats browse in the grassy streets, and dogs and shepherds keep watch from the empty doorways.

A BULL FIGHT IN MADRID.

A bull fight reminds us of those exhibitions of the Colosseum, to which the populace crowded, on the holidays of Rome. The city of Madrid was unusually animated, on the afternoon when we witnessed that cruel sport. The streets were filled with a confused throng, driving, riding, and on foot.

Some were in carriages, with arms and coronets on the panels, and liveried lackeys behind. In little gigs, painted like tea boxes, with a seat for one, containing five; and the driver running by the side. In cabs, with calico tops, and seats and bottoms made of matting. In omnibuses, drawn by mules shaved like Moslem heads, and covered with red tassels and brass bells. On horses, with long flowing tails, stepping with the grace of true Cordovian barbs. On donkeys, wagging their long ears over their innocent noses and dejected eyes; humble as politicians broken down.

Pedestrians in various costumes; mingling silk and rags; breathing garlic and cologne. Lovely senoritas, with round warm faces, with mantillas instead of bonnets, and fans for parasols. Men in cloaks and shawls, with hats in the shape of turbans, embroidered jackets, leathern gaiters, and sashes of red or yellow. Some merely in shirts, and muslin breeches reaching to the knees. Some gaily dressed with straps and eye-glass, like the last pictures in the tailor shops. Little boys, and little girls, running loose, or carried in the arms. Old people, without teeth; beggars and cripples, with their sores and filth. Water carriers, with tin cases and clay jars; street dancers, with castanets; street sweepers and their brooms. Mule barbers, with shears in their girdles. Shepherds in sheepskins, from the mountains; policemen, with feathered hats; blind harpers; distracted strangers; brigands in disguise.

All were passing onward, through the many sultry avenues, out the city gates, to the scene of blood and danger; to applaud or hiss a poor dumb beast, or more pitiable man. The seats around the enclosure, rising like stairs, were soon filled. Thirteen thousand heads were piled one above another; moving as many tongues in shouts and laughter; and twice as many eyes, for curiosity or conquest. There were opera curls and opera glasses; white gloves and white cravats; the waving of colored paper fans; and the smoke of paper segars; and the cries of hucksters, vending fire, oranges and water. There was the royal box, with rich curtains; unoccupied, for the Queen was indisposed. Next to it, sat the Governor of the town and his council. All along were deputies, ministers, high military officers, noblemen, and ambassadors—the blood and distinction of the city.

The sand was sprinkled, soon to be stained. Now a trumpet sounds. A dozen men enter—some on foot, richly clad in silk and gold, with colored mantles on their arms—three mounted, with their legs in iron greaves, and blunt lances, made to wound, not kill. A subordinate, in short black cloak and ostrich plumes, receives a key from the Acalde.

Another trumpet—and the bull bounds from his dark den into the arena. He quivers at first with fear; or is bewildered by the sudden light, and the uproar of the scene. Provoked by the matadores, who close around him their dazzling shawls, he lashes his sides; paws the dust; his red eyes glare defiance, and with a terrific roar, he rushes headlong amongst his foes. But in vain.

They leap out of his course; or on his back; or over the barrier; or throw a cloak on his head. More furious from vexation, he plunges towards a horseman— nor stops for the lance which pierces his shoulder—nor turns aside for the cunning mantle, until he buries his huge horns in the warm body of the steed; tossing him and his rider, like toys, upon the ground.

Then ensues a sight which makes one sick at heart. The wounded beast is remounted, and urged on afresh. The blood is flowing audibly from his gored chest; or still worse, his ragged bowels hang dripping from his side; or trail along the sand, until torn away by the tramp of his own hoofs—and he falls—a shocking, mangled mass; besmearing the rider and the ring with his reeking corpse.

The bull is diverted to an opposite quarter, and attacks another horse. He throws him backward on his haunches; or breaks his leg; or rips the hide half off his breast; or gives him a mortal thrust; that he rears, springs, and dies. Thus he may have killed a fourth or fifth; when weary and weak; with bleeding neck and lolling tongue; familiar with the game; content with triumph, he stands at bay; and awaits, but does not court the combat.

The crowd become impatient, and the trumpet sounds. Bearded darts, in painted papers, are daringly and dexterously planted in his shoulders. These, charged with percussion powder, instantly explode, but still cling to the hide, and sting him to madness. He jumps; tosses his head; bellows with rage and pain; strikes against the barrier; leaps on or over it, and stamps amongst the carcasses around him, till he is almost exhausted.

Again, there is a signal. The matadore bowing to the Director, pale with excitement; or flush with confidence, like an ambitious player, approaches to perform the closing act. A successful blow may win a mistress, a fortune, or a name. A blunder may cause his death; will provoke the hooting of the mob, and throw confusion on his hopes.

Long he shakes his crimson shawl, and points his glittering spear, and often strikes in vain. The wary brute becomes aggressive, and sometimes nearly victor. But in an instant, the steel point appears beneath the shoulder—it is not fatal—another weapon is sheathed in his body—yet he still carries them, and still stands unconquered, though failing from half a hundred wounds.

Another blow and the last. The blood spouts from his nostrils—he groans—he reels—he stumbles—he falls! The matadore bows—the people shout—ladies wave their handkerchiefs—and mules, with flags and ribbons, haul away the carcasses, amidst the lively strains of martial music.

Thus battle after battle proceeds. Perhaps a dozen horses, and half as many bulls are slain, before the sun goes down on this barbarian sport; and the burning of the paper fans, and the final blast of the bugle, tell when the satiated crowd retire.

THE ORIENT.

A fascination has always been connected with the East. It is the "morning land," where Aurora with her rosy fingers opens the gates of day. Whence the light of knowledge and religion first beamed upon the world. Where the human race was cradled—society formed—government organized—the ground first tilled—property acquired—labor paid—nature studied—truth adored.

Towards it, commerce has ever been seeking new routes. To it, military ambition has always tended for glory and dominion. It is endeared to us by the story books of childhood; by the delicious coloring of romance; by the honest claims of history; by the miracles of God.

It has been described as a land of songs and birds, of bards and seers, of love and indolence—where the skies are pearl, the waters nectar, the forests perfume, the winds music—

"Where the virgins are lovely as the roses they twine,
And all, save the spirit of man is divine."

The traveler realizes a different picture. He finds desolation as well as abundance; a luxurious climate, but a wretched civilization; dark, dull countenances, and strange customs which never alter. Every thing tends to surprise him. There, boys and girls of twelve years old marry without love; and the dead are buried without coffins. The people sit on their ancles, sleep in their clothes; and carry their bed on their arm. They have no prejudice against color, and none against dirt. They dig the earth with their hands, and wash clothes with their feet. Many of them have only one eye, and only nine fingers. The servant runs ahead of the master, and the donkey is driven by the tail. The currency is in specie, the lowest coin is worth one fifth of a cent; and the laborer is paid a sixpence a day.

They keep their head covered, but take off their slippers, when they enter a house. Children are carried on the shoulders, and not in the arms; and mourners go about in white. The poor run barefoot; and trades are transmitted with the blood. The butter is made of goat's milk—the bottles of goat's skin. The officials all take bribes; and the law puts a price on crime. Spectacles and umbrellas, are rarely seen; and wheelbarrows are unknown.

The shops have no signs; the streets no sidewalks; the houses no carpets; the fields no fences. The violin has only two strings; and the fiddler, elsewhere, would attract the stones of the streets, but not like Orpheus. They hang pieces of their garments on trees, to cure their maladies. Constables carry whips instead of pistols—the horses wear bells and beads. The bridle bit is shaped like a cross—the stirrups resemble coal shovels—the shoe like a ring covers all the foot, but the frog. The khans, or taverns furnish nothing but chambers and vermin—the guest finds his own couch, and cooks his own meals. He must bargain with the thieves, and pay one, to protect him from the others.

The men wear a sort of petticoat and turbans, instead of hats. The women wear a sort of trowsers, and veils instead of bonnets. The latter dye their nails and eyes, to make them handsome. The former shave their heads, to make them cool. Both sexes smoke—neither chews, tobacco. Everybody likes ottar of roses, and everybody smells of garlic.

The windows are seldom glazed with glass. They thresh grain by driving a sled over the sheaves. They grind flour, by hand, in a mortar. The carpenter holds the board which he saws, by his toes. Nobody is industrious, but the flies and the fleas. None are independent, but the dogs. None are useful, but the camels and asses.

ORATION ON THE 22d FEBRUARY, 1848.

It is not without diffidence, that one rises in so large and enlightened a presence—blest with gallantry and beauty, gay colors, and sweet music—gathered from no compulsory influence; from no motive of sectional interest, or sectarian prejudice, or party policy, or personal advantage. But met from the spontaneous impulse of hearts, exhilirated with patriotic associations; to commemorate the noblest example of humanity which the world ever displayed.

Admiration for whatever is great and good, is a prominent attribute of the human mind. Pure in its source, and salutary in its influence, it gives a redeeming charm to man's fallen nature, and measurably counteracts his continual proclivity to evil and error. It is as universal as reflection. It is witnessed in every period of social progress, and every stage of individual development. It glows like a flame in the buoyant breast of youth, and warms with enthusiasm the failing faculties of age. Communities and countries feel its control, and acknowledge it, by manifestations the most signal, and conspicuous.

This holiday proclaims and illustrates the principle. It is living evidence, and will be through coming years, of national regard for virtue. Its observance gives a perpetual promise to worth, and an incessant spur to duty. It teaches, with an authority more potent than the schools, with an eloquence more magical than man's, the true philosophy of life. It addresses every sense; arrests the usual course of thought; revives or creates impressions of brilliant events; recalls for contemplation a character, which has wrung fame from the misanthrope and the cynic; which has received unanimous and unqualified applause, and formed an era, and remains a model, in the history of the race.

Great qualities had been observed before. Great achievements had been accomplished in every field of human energy and devotion, and the earth was dotted with monuments to great names. There had been patriotism which immolated the heart that cherished it —courage, which sought danger as the wassailer seeks the revel and the bowl—virtue, which passed like the prophet, in triumph, through the flames—genius, which seemed to survey the intellectual world, as with the vision of an angel. Yet, these were isolated traits, or mixed with wrong, or cursed with baser passions.

But here, was an unalloyed concentration of the useful elements of human nature. Such as men had imagined, yet of whose reality they had never been assured. The past is sought in vain—wherever occasion had required or exhibited great powers—the grove, the portico, the agora, the temple, the games, the triumph, the palace, the senate; even ancient Olympus itself, trembling with the innumerable thrones of mortals deified, yielded no type nor fellow.

Heroes before had flourished and perished. Some had written their deeds in blood; forged their names in fire; cast down great empires. Some had framed wise rules of civil action, to unite and preserve communities. Some had charmed mankind by beautiful embodiments of imagination, and thrilling descriptions of feelings, thoughts and truths. Some had lifted the veil from physical mysteries, and displayed the sublime theology of nature. But no other, than our own national father had been so proved in emergency; in peril; in toil; in temptation—had done such precious service—had accomplished so much, so well.

Positive and pre-eminent in his merits, he appeared to unite all the charms and graces with which the muse loves to adorn her creations. In him, were illustrated the wisest maxims of the teachers, and the purest precepts of the books. Faults in man to be expected, in him, had no place. Traits of excellence, rare alone, were in him, combined; and their rays happily blending in one radiant glow, shone like a miracle, attesting the mission he was charged with. He was, indeed, a living revelation; and the seals of his authority were with him; impressed upon his life by the very autograph of God.

He was to be an example at which reproach could not point its finger; which envy could not depreciate; by which ambition might learn the lesson of benevolence; pride, the merit of humility; and truth be justified of her offspring. He was to harmonize discordant sentiments; direct wayward sympathies to a single object; inspire capability with faith in itself; unite in a common cause, with a simultaneous impulse, energies distracted and conflicting; and retrieve the lost sovereignty of individual man. He was to be an instrument of political salvation.

Before his influence was felt, every government had failed to promote the common weal. Every kind of rule, which avoided oppression, was unfit to protect. Power was the companion of tyranny. Liberty and security appeared to be incompatible.

The masses exercised no rights: and their whole duty was submission. They were without responsibility, and without choice. No provision was made for their interest; no consideration was given to their opinion. Their claims to participation were treated with derision. Their prayers for relief were rebuked by accumulated wrong. Justice, withheld its dues; charity, its allowance. If they had not suffered, they should have resisted. If their condition had been easy, it was yet degrading; for it implied the principle of subjection, and acknowledged their incapacity.

But these relations were to be changed. The world had grown wiser and better. It became actuated by new spirits, and practical aims. The temple gates of knowledge had been wide open flung; and the common mind had entered. New sentiments were developed and diffused; information was scattered abroad; the bread had been cast upon the waters, and the time of its gathering was at hand.

Signal results appeared; an altered order of events followed. Fictions, gave way to facts; words, to things; students of the cloister, to students of the world; schoolmen to statesmen. The doctrine of equal rights was investigated and asserted. The presumption of the dominant few was assailed. Sacrifices were anticipated without alarm, and endured without regret.

Death was deemed milder than tribute; life was not to be compared with principle.

Force, wealth, birth, station, and prescription no longer constituted pre-eminence. Badges, the robe, the mitre, the crown, the sword became equally disregarded and despised, as the emblems of merit, and the means of control. The superstitions, which time had almost hallowed; the prejudices of the throne; the bigotry of the church, declined. The mystery which invested ancient forms; the obscurity which concealed ancient error, disappeared. The explosion of false dogmas, and the wholesome effects of contending castes and creeds, succeeded.

On a new soil arose the struggle of republicanism. Society was shaken with the strife of hostile systems and relations. Returning gloom and confusion threatened to prevail. The genius of Washington moved over the troubled elements. A new political creation dawned.

It seemed adapted to the requirements of the time. It concided with the changed habitudes of thought; with the improved notions of right; with the new political nature of man. It presented a theatre of influence extensive and attractive; uncursed with the trammels of custom; untainted with the breath of tyranny; where faith and freedom joined their altars, and mingled their blessings; where the foundations of glorious institutions were laid; where a hopeful community was planted, to expand and flourish for ages.

Look around, for it is here—it is ours, upon the seat and operation of its energies. Protected by wide seas from the perplexing interference of alien and unfriendly powers. Covering an area which surpasses in extent the territory of all the chief nations of antiquity.

Grooved with rivers in which all the navies of the world could ride. Girt with a sea coast stretching one fourth of the circuit of the globe. Yielding infinite facilities for exchange and intercourse. Displaying the beauty of every scenery; the fertility of every soil; minerals of every mark; the flowers of the East; the luxuries of the line; valleys lovely as Yemen; shores prolific as the Nile; the roses of Palestine; the orchards of Persia; the cane fields of Jamaica; the vineyards of the Rhine; the gold of India; the iron of Britian; the marble of Pentelicus.

With such extraordinary advantages from nature is our country blessed. With an origin not confused in the gloom of fable, nor stained by criminal success; but creditable, fortunate, and manifest. With a history so brief, yet so illustrious. Still in the period of national youth, yet performing prodigies in skill and valor. And now at a time of unwonted activity, when earth rings with the ceaseless noise of enterprise and toil—she appears like the leader of the nations, cheering them with her voice and example, as they marvel at her march, and crowd upon her wake. Joy attends her at every step; obstacles sink before her; success crowns her efforts. She counsels with the wisdom of Minerva; she labors with the hand of Hercules; she fights with the sword of Mars.

See the results of her power, in the cities she has reared along the banks of waters, and on the plains; embellished with every charm which taste desires, or opulence can furnish; and murmuring with the ever grateful echo of employment and content. And in the channeled mountains, the artificial tides, the iron roads and iron steed; the harvest whitening on the site of the wilderness; learning sought where ignorance had spread its pall; religion kneeling on the grave of idols.

And in her armies of citizen soldiers, instinct with valor as with the love of country and feelings of honor; intelligent and cultivated; the source of prosperity in peace, and their career in battle stranger than fiction. No records, no fables match them; resistless as the sea; forward from field to field, like fate; wrenching victory from surpassing force, from impregnable walls. And kind as fierce; as merciful by the litter of the wounded, as terrible in the ridges of battle; lenient in the midst of rage; sparing in the hour of revenge. And this day, a year ago, in the fatal vale of Angostura, the American volunteer, amidst the crashing of bones, and the red gush of blood, expressed an energy and a soul, which have crowned the name with everlasting laurel.

These are the legitimate consequences of national institutions and habits—of those fundamental principles, which recognize the existence of absolute rights, and individual independence. Unspeakably happy may we be, that our lot has been cast in a country so highly favored as our own. Possessing, as it does, all the materials of power in union; the security of freedom in universal interest and responsibility; in the prevalence of christian morals, and the spread of letters. While the certainty of reward and the confidence of protection, insure the display of effort, the progress of art, the perfection of means, and the accumulation of wealth.

It is the land of Washington, immeasurably blessed and famous by his birth and deeds. A land of great works and changes—of free discussion—of healthful excitement—of active curiosity—of remarkable results. A land of steam, of lightning—of commerce, of invention—of liberality, of sympathy, of knowledge—of religious toleration, of missionary zeal, of civil equality, of female influence—of the bible, of the press, of the schoolmaster. A land of public opinion.

But not such opinion as in other places, and at different periods, affected the customs and conditions of people. Not such as at one time, regarded Polytheism with favor; physical courage as the highest virtue; and suicide as an honorable death. Not such as received, with reverence and faith, prophetic declarations from the Pythian tripod; or conformed the course of enterprise to the conventional omens of elements and brutes. Not such as imputed merit to the magician's wand, or read in the necromantic mirror of the future, the fortunes of characters and countries. Not such as encouraged the fierce fanaticism of the Koran and the Crusades. Not such as upheld the terrors of the Inquisition, or the military tyranny of the feudal system; as fostered the delirious spirit of chivalrous adventure, turning life into romance with the gay tournaments of Templars, and the amorous roundelays of Troubadours. Not such as tolerated torture amongst the punishments of criminal law; or ordeals by fire and water amongst its methods of trial; or applauded the reckless blasphemy of the Cyclopedists, or maintained the orthodoxy of indulgences, the pretensions of rank, or the divine prerogaative of Kings.

But an opinion, formed by universal reflection, and criticism—the aggregate judgment of mankind—the public conscience of the world, qualified and enlightened by the influence of christian revelation. Comprehending and sustaining the appropriate relation of things; the principles of rights and obligations; the interests and responsibilities of life. Speaking with a spontaneous and united effort, approving whatever promotes; and denouncing whatever opposes human happiness

Our country thus upheld by such a moral force; by constitutional provisions of equal operation and general advantage; and by the prompt and matchless prowess of her children—we can prescribe no limits to her progress; and patriotism, may dream of continual duration, and universal fame. Of the time, when she shall control and direct the course and destiny of civilized society. When her commerce shall be vaster than all which Venice had, and Albion has, combined. When the productions of her handicraft shall be more reputed than those of the Sidonian artists. When her soldiers shall accomplish more than the Roman or the Gaul. When her orators shall leave loftier models than the Greek or Saxon. When her bards shall sing diviner melodies than his, whose muse soared above the Aonian Mount; or his, the blind Maeonides of seven cities claimed.

And her flag shall float on every wave, and in every wind, representing the purest government and happiest people; the emblem of political faith and redemption to millions, wrestling in the darkness and debasement of oppression. And her voice shall ever nerve the timid; cheer the feeble; sever the bonds; break the yokes; fling wide the prison doors; open the blinded eyes; unseal the silent lips, till the world rings with pæans to her praise. And there shall be no darkness in her future; no failing in the vigor of her institutions; no change in her original principles; no bounds to her development and growth, to the trophies of her toil and arms; no halting in her brilliant course, till her rivers cease to flow, and her iron hills shall fade; and freedom, and time, and she, with a common fate, expire together.

Such anticipations fill us with thrilling reflections; stimulate every patriotic propensity; expand our charities; elevate our sentiments; argue against our frailty, and flatter our pride. But prospects so gratifying may be delusive. Decay, with her ashy fingers, seems to have written ruin on everything of human skill. Nations, like those who compose them, appear to be born with the doom of dissolution—to flourish for awhile and then pass away.

Such is the lesson of experience,

> "And the moral of all human tales,
> 'Tis but the same rehearsal of the past!
> First freedom, then glory! when that fails,
> Wealth, vice, corruption—barbarism at last.
> And history, with all her volumes vast,
> Hath but one page."

Desolation and mystery reign over the courts and pylones of Luxor and Karnak, and the mausolea of the Pharaohs. The satyr and the bittern possess the halls and palaces, in which the Assyrian nobles had their orgies, and Belus his smoking altars. The lonely fisherman dries his net on the rocks, where the Tyrian merchants heaped up purple and gold. Degeneracy and ruin mark the city, where the Athenian gazed with rapture on the temple of his tutelar goddess, decorated by the chisel of Phidias and the pencil of Zeuxis; or beheld justice issuing, pure as heaven, from the hill of Mars; or witnessed Socrates illustrating the virtuous philosophy he taught; or heard and believed the eloquence of Pericles proclaiming the state immortal. Lazaroni lead the pensive stranger over hillocks of crushed columns and sculptured fragments; seeking the ways along which Cæsar's legions passed with spoil and captives; or the temple walls, in which Tully last harangued the Conscript fathers. Gone is the dynasty of the Abassides; and the glory of Bagdad, whose long caravans daily left her gates, to distribute the intellectual treasures of her students, and the costly wares of her cunning workmen.

These nations had not, indeed, the instruction which their own, and succeeding experiments, have yielded. They had not our facilities of travel and communication. They had not heard, or heeded the voice which, by the seashore and the wayside, by Genesareth, and on the mountain, preached the new kingdom of love. But their systems were defective, because they were human—and ours of like original, may share their fate. But when, or how—by choice or chance; by foreign or internal force or fraud; by sudden or continued injury; by luxury or by ambition—no Sibyl leaves can tell, no oracle can answer.

She may fall by her own hand; a sacrifice upon her own altar; the victim of her own shame; the spoil of her own passions. She may fall in the prime of vigor;

amidst the wildest convulsions, amidst the tumult of tumbling thrones and senates, and the conflict and blood of extended revolution. Her sun may go down in clouds and storm, "casting disastrous" darkness o'er the nations—it may go down in light, splendid to the last, its beams long illuminating the firmament it leaves forever.

But by restraining the license of party spirit; by the exercise of vigilant care over the elective privilege; by the untrammeled administration of jurisprudence; by giving unremitting attention to mental cultivation, and unfailing recompense to works of art and acts of merit; by inculcating a rational reverence for the day of holy rest; and the practice and precepts of Christian worship, this nation will be a blessing to countless generations, who in succession will fill our places.

Then let her cling to her early virtues; let her embrace only that which will exalt her; let her extend her dominion only to enlighten; let her fight only in the cause of truth and honor; let her achieve deeds fit to be stamped in stone or graved in gold; let her become a "comforter of the earth;" and eventful centuries shall pass, and great cycles revolve while she endures. Incalculably distant will be the period, when she must yield to the inevitable order of creation; and pay her last reluctant tribute to the universal law of change.

ALEXANDRIA AND CAIRO.

The stranger in Alexandria is confused at first by the shouting mob, masked women, stalls full of trifles, complexions from straw to ebony, languid eyes, long beards, bald heads, red caps, loose blouses, soldiers in white flowing trousers; carriages, with servants on foot; Moslem Hadjis, half clad, and half starved.

Palm trees are in the suburbs and villages, with low, flat roofs. Heifers turn huge water wheels to irrigate the Pasha's garden. Markets are in the open air, supplied with bread made of dates, sugar cane in stalks, beans and pigeons, wheat at forty cents a bushel, and hideous black slaves. The streets are baked hard as tiles. The sun glows like a furnace. The slender minarets rise here and there. The crescent floats over the city.

The ancient ruins, are chiefly beneath the sand. The catacombs in the subterranean rocks are difficult of access, and swarm with bats. There is scarcely any conspicuous remains of the great city, which was a second Tyre for commerce; rivaled Athens in learning, and Rome in wealth. An unfluted column, with a Corinthan capital, known as Pompey's pillar, stands upright near the sea.. A prostrate obelisk, and some parts of baths, are only left of the palaces of Cleopatra; that voluptuous queen, who charmed the prudent heart of Cæsar—seduced Anthony from war and power, to love and ruin—who fascinated, like a sorceress—

> "Whom age could not wither,
> Nor custom stale her infinite
> Variety."

Cario, the old city of the Caliphs, has a more oriental character. It contains many mosques, to whose number, each succeeding Pasha adds another. All have fountains for ablution; and some are of costly marble, and alabaster, but of shabby workmanship. Some are crumbling down, but their decay, sacred as the errors they enshrine, cannot be disturbed.

The Palace has furniture of silk and porcelain, stone baths, fountains and slaves. The citadel overlooks the town, and is famous for the massacre, and the giddy leap, of the last of the Mamelukes. The well, called Joseph's is sunk a prodigious depth, with an inclined pathway to the bottom. The Bazaars are filled with amber tubes, cherry pipe stems, and red Fez caps. The quarters of the city are divided by gates, and devoted to separate trades. The pleasant gardens are odorous with the fumes of aromatic coffee and tobacco. A few rough carts wabble along the streets, on wheels which have no tires. Infant jugglers, gymnastic monkeys, and snake charmers exhibit at the corners. Ovens are contrived to supersede hens in hatching chickens. An agate forest covers the neighboring sands with petrified trunks and branches, heavy as iron.

Howling Dervishes, a moslem sect, worship by vibrating their heads, like pendulums, and grunting in concert, like an orchestra of brutes. The law compels every person abroad at night to carry a lantern. A towel is hung over the doors of public baths, during the hours they are occupied by women. A Mecca guide, with long hair and beard, in red trowsers, and naked to the waist—sometimes passes along, amidst the respectful salutations of the crowd. Abbas Pasha, with his eyes almost closed by fat, and his other features not indicative of genius, occasionally drives by in a phaeton; preceded by riders, who clear the street with lashes. The Copts show, for a consideration, their Coptic bible, and poverty stricken church; built, as they say, over the tomb of Abraham. The Latin monks have a convent in which they treat strangers with genuine hospitality.

But this is still fanatic Egypt; where superstition has her seat, and magic and false prophets have long had dominion over human faith. Some little evidence, however, appears of improving times. Trifles, like straws, show the course of currents. Some European clothes; some christian women's faces; some sign-boards, in Roman letters; some foreign hotels, and foreign bankers, and the increase of travel, foreshadow the encroachment of a better policy, and a wiser creed.

THE NILE.

Behold the Nile! the joy of the Arab! the mother of Egypt! annually overflowing! a thousand miles without a tributary stream! Swelling proudly along its fertile sides, as if conscious of its prolific virtue and old renown! Coming from that much sought, and long undiscovered country—the abode, perhaps, of some patriarchal tribe; or some savage horde; some virgin wilderness; or some fairy land; which poets have long dreamed of, and travelers toiled, and Cæsar sighed for, in the very arms of victory and love!

It was once said to flow from heaven. It was deemed divine and worshiped. A beautiful maid was every year its sacrificial feast. On its delightful banks, great Jove himself was wont to spend some summer days.

From its famous valley, doubtless sprang those once popular mythologies; those

"Gay religions full of pomp and gold."

Those schemes of human worship, which warmed the fancy of the classic bards. They had some little truth debased with infinite errors. Deities subordinate, and supreme, imbued with human frailties; divinities of war, and love, and wine; the soul immortal, but itinerant amongst brutes and birds; or borne over Charon's ferry to the realms of Pluto; ceremonies of prayer and propitiation, but to idols foul; altars such as stirred the spirit of Paul in Athens, inscribed in ignorance to the unknown God.

It was here, also, science must have had its cradle. Here nations learned their alphabets and numerals. Hence armies, colonies and scholars went forth to subdue, and educate, and distribute civilization through the world. Here were schooled the gifted of the Greeks. Here Solon studied the principles of legislation; Plato, the systems of philosophy; Pythagoras, the true theory of the planetary revolutions; Thales, how to calculate eclipses; Eratosthenes, how to measure the circumference of the globe; the Father of history, the art of composing annals; the Prince of poets, the glorious measure of the epic muse.

A cruel barbarian destroyed the last written vestiges of that learning, in which the Jewish lawgiver was imbued; and which must have charmed, perhaps, corrupted the uxorious soul of Solomon. Those countless scrolls of papyrus, which heated for months the Moslem baths, may have been inscribed with learning, with songs, and eloquence, worthy of the mighty monarchy of Rhamses.

But elements and barbarism have assailed, but not destroyed the pyramids. Grand as nature, their forms eternal as their rocks; they seem more like mountains than masonry. Nor were they built in vain. Though their founders' names are lost, and the carcasses they covered, scattered; they are yet conspicuous evidence of accumulated wealth; of regulated labor; of cultivated genius. They are memorials of established government, and civil law. They are monuments of society, and civilization, the oldest in the world.

They were there, before that wise Judean king took thence that royal bride, in whose honor, they say, he built a city. Before Pharaoh's gentle daughter, bathing in those waters, found the infant Moses in his cradle ark. The chosen children must have beheld them, when they served in those neighboring fields. Joseph must have passed them, when, arrayed in fine linen vestures and the chain of gold, he rode in the second chariot of the land. Abraham must have looked upon them, when sojourning there with Sarah, whose beauty charmed the nobles and the monarch. Men may have seen them, who walked the earth with Noah. Their builders may have heard the subsiding waters of the deluge; and raised them, to be beyond the reach of future ruin.

For forty centuries they have stood. Millions have passed beneath their shadows.—strangers and slaves; kings and crowds; in infinite procession. Empires have followed one another in these plains, like scenes upon a stage. Fair cities have risen on those banks, and disappeared, and scarcely left a wreck of their foundations. A single prostrate statue, nearly shrouded in the sand, is all that remains of the once polished Memphis. A lone obelisk stands, like a grave-stone, over the site of ancient On.

Those mute piles have witnessed all their hopes and fates—their splendor and their desolation. They may still long endure; and survive other scenes and undeveloped changes, until earth's final hour. And as they are the earliest, they may be the last remains of man.

The largest occupies thirteen acres of ground; contains several small chambers; an empty sarcophagus; and has an opening of 26° to the horizon, which pointed at the time of its construction, to the polar star. Its sides are crumbling, but it is sustained by granite corner stones, thirty and forty feet long, and two or three feet high. Up these tall steps you are rapidly elevated by importunate guides, four hundred and fifty feet, to the apex. There, on a platform of thirty feet square, you may dine; carve your name in the soft stone; gaze over the dreary sand, or down the ragged sides upon the marred and broken spinx, whose colossal paws, fifty feet in length, inclose a buried temple; or you may watch the Arabs as they perform, without lifting their feet, a native dance, on the top of this sepulchre of a king or god.

Musing on these old wonders; in a barge far different from hers, whose silken sails and gilded masts floated down the Cydnus; drinking a beverage, Horace wanted, when he journeyed to Brundusium; feeding on fishes without scales, which Lucullus would have loved; you wind up the river for many days. The skies are seldom clouded; delicious mingling of blue and purple skirts the horizon as the sun goes down. The night comes on at once, with scarcely any twilight, and the stars convert the canopy into a dome of diamonds.

A double range of sandy mountains run parallel on the opposite shores, inclosing this pleasant region, which for beauty and fertility, seems the very paragon of countries. There are sections of sugar cane, divided by gutters; tracts of cotton, like fields of fleece; acres of mustard, and winds light and warm blow

"Sabean odours from the spicy shores
Of Araby the blest."

The sight delighted, wanders over a strangely contrasted landscape—meadows in every stage of cultivation; the glebe fresh turned; the grain fresh sprouted; the blossom's bloom; the fruit matured. The plowman and the sower; the reaper and he that gathereth up the sheaves, go side by side. Seed time and harvest are in one day, and in one plain,

" Spring and autumn dancing hand in hand."

There are rocky cliffs in some places near the water, abrupt and high, from whose top the eagle screams; in whose sides the wild fowls build. There are cranes, ranked like an army on the beach, as numerous as those that warred upon the pigmies. There are crowds of pelicans, white as wool, and grave as juries; flocks of geese gliding on the river, wheeling through the air, or waddling on the ground, shy as maids. A pair of crocodiles lie sleeping on the shore, with their guardian birds to warn them of danger, and pick their teeth for pay.

Droves of buffaloes, with ram-like horns, are tethered in the grass, or playing with all their might, as they gallop to the bank for drink. There are large cows from Nubia, with humps like saddles, on their shoulders; herds of sheep, with naked children for their shepherds; strings of camels laden with wares for the interior; or spices for the cities; groves of date trees, with leaves like ostrich feathers; the grateful shade of gum arabic;

the desert, wide and waste over which the sandy whirlwinds dance.

There are villages of sun-dried bricks, from whose minarets, the priests call to prayers; women in blue slips, washing or carrying water on their heads in earthen jars; men irrigating the soil, nude as nature, of whom it may be said: " they owe the worm no silk, the beast no hide, the sheep no wool, the cat no perfume." There are numerous boats with sails like swallow's wings, freighted with corn or cotton, or slaves from the line; rafts of pottery joined by green palm ropes, floating down to market.

There are the pylones and courts of Thebes:

> "The world's great mistress on the Egyptian plains."

The ruins of palaces and temples, sculptured and painted with history and fable, are vast as cities; as if their founders had been giants; or as Champollion says, one hundred feet in height; or as the Arabs speak, tall as the palm trees; as if their lives had been measured by centuries; and like the Titans, they were able to cope with the Gods themselves.

Though these remains are disfigured, and occupied by entire mud villages; by the accumulated rubbish of ages; by myriads of pigeons; poisonous reptiles; and burrowing foxes, yet no one can regard their huge dimensions, unsubdued. Walls stand, on whose top carriages could pass. Obelisks of a single stone, slender and pointed, rise eighty feet upright. Lofty columns are counted by hundreds. Statues are seen nearly a thousand tons weight, and twenty feet across the shoulders. Memnon, fabled to have saluted the rising sun with music, and which still echoes like metal to a blow; is fifty feet above the sand, though seated. It is only one of a double colonnade which once formed an avenue two miles in length.

Compared to such relics, all other antiquites and structures dwindle into toys. What magnificent scenes they once witnessed! when the inclosures were perfect; the courts paved; shining with pleasant furniture; the pillars all upright; the decorations fresh; the avenues crowded; the altars fuming with sacrifice!

But time and enemies have spent their rage upon this famous city,

"She who stretched her conquest o'er a thousand States;"

Whose rulers were the chief of warriors; whose priests were the sages of the world; whose people were the first of nations; the city of poetry and prophecy; of Homer's verse and Ezekiel's vision, has been rent asunder; as it was written; and her multitudes, cut off, fill the mountains with their mummies and their tombs.

THE DESERT.

Our caravan was composed of several camels, and each one's nose was tied to the tail of the one it followed. Some were loaded with canvas, water, cooking pans, and poultry. My dragoman, who was a Copt in religion, a mulatto in complexion, and a very promiscuous rascal, had the use of another. I rode on one, in a sort of palanquin, furnished with pipes, lunch, and water in leathern bottles. The drivers, a sheik in green turban, and his man, generally walked, often in their barefeet, and when the ground was too hot, they wore sandals.

It was in the middle of April when we left the Nile—those pleasant shores where the summer never fails, and the rain never falls. We passed the plains of Goshen, once the seat of Joseph's kindred, blooming with fruits and grain. We reached a small village in the evening, and to avoid thieves, encamped in a cow-yard, amongst fleas and other carniverous insects. This reminded us of the proverb of Scylla and Charybdis.

We were, however, early on the way, moving directly towards the sun, as his beams reddening, and spreading up the horizon, burst forth in floods of fire. Slowly and steadily we traveled onward, without pause, or turning, dining as we rode; over the hard, over the yielding surface, until the night. The baggage was unloaded, the charcoal kindled, the tent pitched, and I supped alone as usual on coffee, and chickens, partly boiled, by the partly civilized cook. The meal was more symbolical than palatable.

The camels were fed on beans, the men had their repast, and all lay down and slept outside of the canvas. I strolled some rods away. The air was calm, but cool. The moon in her silver mask was climbing the azure dome. The eastern stars followed in glittering procession. Their mellow light shed a pleasant influence over the vast and solitary wild.

All sublunary nature seemed at rest. No rustle of reeds, no buz of wings, no fall of footsteps, no purl of stream informed the listening sense. I could perceive neither form of living creature, nor noise of living breath, except my own. But there was, withal, an exterior sound; indistinct and unaccountable, subdued, yet unsuppressed. It was continuous; like the roaring of a shell, or the rushing of a wind, or the distant voice of the sea, or the confused murmurs of a city. But it could have arisen from no such sources. Could it be an imaginary impression? Could silence thus produce an illusion on the ear, as darkness sometimes does upon the eye? Or was it the aggregate respiration of unseen life—the whirring movement of sleepless spirits—the secret pulses of the world—the mysterious harmonies of the universe. Philosophers may seek its cause. Arabs are satisfied with calling it, the silence of the desert.

The next day or two, our course lay over an undulating tract of hill and vale. We suffered from the uneasy motion of the camel, which does not make one sick but sore, and which none but a Bedouin can long endure. The fierce sun burned relentlessly above us. Neither rock, nor tree, nor cloud interposed a grateful shadow. The sky was brass, the earth iron. The Sirocco blew its tropical breath hot as flames.

By some extravagance, our food was diminished, and the supply of water exhausted. The mirage shone like a lake before us, and fled our approach, as water once the lips of Tantalus. We then remembered well, as whilom did wandering Israel, the flesh pots, the fishes and the sweet river of Egypt. Some days, the fine sand drove against us in furious waves, stifling, blinding and scorching as they passed. Our poor beasts of burthen, wearied or alarmed, turned at last abruptly around, and refused to proceed.

We dismounted; the tent raised, was once blown over, and with difficulty secured against the gale.

Lying down within its oven-like shelter, I was soon enveloped in a drift of dust, which had penetrated through the pores of the canvas. We resumed the journey after nightfall. There soon appeared approaching toward us, in the dim moonlight, a long string of camels with riders, and drivers, filing over the irregular ground. Silently and swiftly they came; nearer and nearer; until we were about to salute them, when—they vanished like a phantom! and we never saw them more.

The next day, we arrived at one of those cisterns, dug, in certain places, for the benefit of wanderers, and which collect and retain the rains of the spring. A large stone hand was on it; and near it, were the prints of a horse's hoof, made very wide apart by the Arabs, to commemorate the strength and speed of a famous freebooter. He was one of the heroes of their stories;

and born black, though of white parents, in answer to his mother's prayer.

The water was thick with slime; green and fœtid. The men descended; stood in it knee deep, and filled the large goat skins and the bottles. Parched and thirsty, we drank it with avidity.

With no other beverage than this, we went on, for several days, over the empty basins of lakes, shining with incrusted salt. Cool, moist sea breezes soon refreshed us; and we saw at hand the blue tents of other travelers. A Russian Prince, with a large retinue, was bound to the same destination; he furnished us with fresh water; and we pursued the rest of our route together. Some hawks, some daisies, the foot prints of jackals, and a hyena, and the bed of a waterless river, varied the monotony of the way, as we reached a village; the second we had seen since leaving Cairo.

Having paid the usual sum for a watch during the night; we left at dawn, and were soon followed by the Sheik. He demanded extra pay, because we were in two parties. We refused to recognize this ingenious apportionment. The excited sheik shook his shawl, pulled off his sandals, and left us with threats of vengeance. In an hour, he returned, with all the males of the village, armed with guns, clubs and knives. They shouted "baksheesh"—moved towards us—we faced them—a shock seemed certain. But they halted. For although twice as numerous, they observed that some of the Russians were well armed. They then posted themselves in front of us; with all manner of gestures and menaces; but as we advanced, they one by one, stood aside. They next hung on our rear, and on our flank; and for several miles, followed us with noise, and the clatter of their weapons. But baffled and defied, they at last retired. They doubtless assailed us with much vernacular impudence, which as we did not understand, we did not resent.

We passed directly on, here and there, by some prickly grass, which the camels cropped in marching—some modest flowers wasting their virtues—some dreary vales with drifts like snow. After nearly a fortnight's dismal travel, we came, at once, on a plain of boundless green; dotted with numerous tents, black and comely as the tents of Kedar. Droves of camel calves cried after us like children. Busy reapers were bending to the grain. Cool breezes fanned us from the ocean. Deep wells bubbled with fresh water. It was the season of flowers; it was the valley of Sharon; the voice of the turtle; the carol of the lark; and myriads of singing birds made the welkin echo with the sweetest sounds in nature. The day seemed like an hour; the road like a garden path. Old olives were white with vernal bloom. Crimson blossoms shone like leaves of fire amongst the branches of pomegranate trees. There were pinks like stars upon the ground; roses worthy of the Psalmist's songs; lilies such as the delighted eye of Christ remembered, when he uttered the parable of providence.

A transition so unforseen gave us a delicious impression of this, the Holy Land. Other countries have their attractions. You may trace the course of science along the descending Nile—the flight of victory as it followed the Roman eagles—climb the heights of Greece where they invoked the muses. But the soul turns with an immortal interest to Palestine, where the incarnate Deity walked with the children of men.

THE BEDOUIN AND HIS FRIENDS.

The Bedouin is proud of his Chaldean father and Egyptian mother; and though half Gentile and half Jew, he has no sympathy with either. He seems to rejoice in verifying the predicted misanthropy of the seed of Ishmael. His hand is against every man.

He is regarded as an infidel. Indifferent both to Jerusalem and to Meccca—he makes no pilgrimages. Without altars, or temples, or fountains—he makes neither ablutions nor prostrations. He loves the moving stars above him, and the moving sands beneath him. He builds no cities; and holds in contempt the luxury of palaces, the works of art, and the drudgery of labor. He has no schools, is unable to read; yet fond of poetic recitations.

He is governed by hereditary sheiks. He dwells under tents of camel's hair, spread like an awning. He is satisfied with dates, cheese and honey. He moves his abode when the pastures fail. He always goes armed, and mostly with a lance. He wears only a loose blouse around his body, and a small shawl over his head, with which he often conceals his face. His figure is slight, but sinewy; his complexion nearly black; his features regular, but felonious.

He has credit for virtues which he rarely exhibits. He is not too proud to beg, but mean enough to steal.

His hospitality refuses the traveler water without pay. His courage prefers rather to waylay than to fight. He revels in the vast expanse of the desert. It suits the wildness of his spirit, and the sterility of his mind. It affords him an opportunity for plunder, and a refuge from justice. But he is generally true to his contract, and seldom betrays a trust. He avenges with bloodshed, the death of his kindred. The friend whom he admits to his board, may rely on his shelter and his spear. His wealth is not rated in acres, but in stock.

The camel is essential to him. It suits his life, by its unique conformation and habits. It is ugly, and ill shaped, with a long neck and a short tail; but its face is expressive of humility and patience. Its great height affords free play to its limbs, and a commanding view to the rider. Its arched back increases its strength, and capacity to carry. It kneels to be loaded, and refuses to rise when oppressed. Lifting two legs on one side at the same time, it careens, like a ship, in its motions. Its soft, round feet, scarcely sink in the sand. Its gate is regular and steady, at the rate of two miles an hour. It is often as swift as an ostrich. It is scarcely affected by heat, and goes two weeks without water.

It is dangerous when provoked; revengeful as its master, but true to him. It carries him on his journeys; his plunder, when he robs; his merchandize, when he trades; his tent, when he changes his abode; his arms, when he fights; his presents, when he goes a wooing; his bride, when he has wedded. Its body makes him a shelter from the storm, and a shade from the sun. Its flesh yields him food; its hair furnishes his garments.

The Bedouin prizes his camel, but he loves his horse. That noble beast shares his heart with his women and children. He is educated with care. He is inured to fatigue, hunger, and thirst. He is taught to wheel,—to halt at full speed—to evade the lance—to stand fire.

His pedigree can be traced back for generations. He is decked with tassels and amulets. He moves with the pride of heroic blood. He disdains all burthens but his rider. His flowing tail,—his silken mane,—his neck superbly arched,—his lifted feet, seem to combine all the grace and glory of animal life. Such a creature must have inspired the graphic pen of Job, the gratitude of Alexander, the fond folly of Caligula.

The Bedouin esteeming his horse and camel as faithful friends, bears the indifference of a savage to all others.

JERUSALEM.

The interest of Palestine culminates at Jerusalem. There, stood the ancient Salem, from which Melchisideck went forth to bless the Patriarch, returning victorious from the battle, with Lot, his goods and women. There, God spared the son of Abraham, and there, He sacrificed his own. There, the abominations of Canaan, the brutish worship, the fire of Moloch provoked the avenging sword of Israel. There, celestial fire consumed the offering of David on the threshing floor of Ornan. The destroying angel stayed there his arm. Thither, they brought the holy ark with music. There, the glorious temple rose.

The present city, of about fifteen thousand inhabitants, is situated on a precipitous declivity, surrounded on three sides by deep ravines. Its battlemented walls, tall square towers, domes, and infinite white tombs relieve the monotony of a vast, desolate region. All around seems a wilderness of rocks; as if rain had swept away the soil, or fire had burned up the roots of vegetation. Except a few olives, and patches of grass and grain, all else is drear and sterile. No cedars crown the heights with forests. No arable plains appear, nor blooming gardens, nor fragrant orchards.

The lovely scenes, the delightful fields, the sweet flowers which we read of in Eastern tales—the flowing pastures, the sparkling fountains—the land of corn and grapes, and oil, and honey, such as the spies reported, and Moses saw from Pisgah; such as Tacitus, Hecataeus and the Imperial Apostate praised, are there no more. The clusters of Eschol are as scarce as the giants of Anak. Nothing recalls the beauty and abundance of the heathen authors, and the sacred bards. There is no view which charms the sense, no cheerful spot on which the sight delights to linger. Nature seems to have failed, the ground looks wan, the air breathes decay.

There is scarcely left any evidence of former wealth, prosperity, or power. The roads which Solomon's chariots traversed, have disappeared. The aqueducts which supplied the fountains, are here and there discovered by their broken arches. But you may see the pool of Gihon, now dry, built of huge stones, where the beauty of Bathsheba bathing, provoked the guilt of the enamored King. The ancient well of Job, (so named,) one hundred and twenty-five feet deep, still bubbles with pure water. There are the venerable walls of Siloa's brook, "which flowed fast by the Oracle," and now lines the banks with verdure. The tower of Hippicus still stands, huge and square, as it was built by Herod.

There are chambers, with Doric columns, large as bed-rooms, cut in the limestone hills, with sepulchres, such as held the bodies of kings and judges, the Virgin and the Saviour. A crumbling arch remains of the bridge which once united Mounts Zion and Moriah. Great beveled stones, the only reputed relics of the temple, attract the Jews each Friday to bewail the possession of the aliens. Besides these, and Bethesda's pool, now empty, where He bade the cripple walk; there are, perhaps, no other undisputed remains of the ancient city.

But there are natural localities which cannot be mistaken. There is the barren field of blood, bought with the silver which Judas could not keep. And the Mount of Moriah, the site of the temple, covered now by the Mosque of Omar, with its wells, its domes, and tombs, and lamps of ostrich eggs. There is the valley of Kedron, dry until swollen by the winter rains. Above its banks is Gethsemane, inclosing eight old olives, which may have witnessed that bloody agony and prayer, when He asked that the hour and the cup might pass.

Mount Zion, partly ploughed as a field, is the resort of lepers, and full of graves. There are the sloping sides of Olivet; hallowed, by the grief of David, when with covered head and naked feet, he and his people went up, weeping from the parricidal arm of Absalom; and of Jesus, when amidst palms and hosannahs, he sadly gazed upon the city, which stoned the prophets, and wept over its inevitable fate.

There he beheld, in vision, the fell calamity, and heavy woes which followed—the rage of battle; the crash of walls; the terrific flames; the frightful famine; the agony of hunger, turning men and mothers into monsters; the city's fall—the bloodiest in human annals—not a stone left of the sanctuary, itself a wonder—its foundations leveled by the remorseless ploughshare—its site sown with salt. It was from Olivet the Saviour was borne to heaven from his blest disciples; and there he shall first place his feet, when, with his angels and in glory, he returns again.

That easy credulity which delights to locate every incident of interest, points out the mulberry in the valley of Cheesemongers, as the one under which Isaiah was sawn assunder; the grotto in which Jeremiah dwelt; the rock which concealed the disciples; where Stephen was stoned, and James beheaded; where Christ ate the passover on Zion, and brake the bread, and poured the wine, as memorials of his blood and body. They show a rock imprinted by his foot, when he was kissed and bound; the site of his prison, where Peter followed and denied him; where he was clad in scarlet, crowned with thorns, spit upon and smitten. They show where he fainted, as he bore his cross, followed by those gentle women, whom he bade weep for themselves and children.

There, covering the supposed site of Calvary, is a large church, whose origin is attributed to the dream and piety of Helena. It is garnished by the gorgeous gifts of generations, and occupied by the various sects of christianity. Within it, the foresight of the Monks claims to have discovered every eventful spot. A plate in one place, marks the centre of the world, from which the dust of Adam's body was obtained. Near to this, three bright rings are sunk in the floor, where Christ was crucified between the thieves. In another part, the soldiers cast lots for the unseamed garment. A fissure in the rock was rent, they say, when darkness and earthquake convinced the Roman that the Son of God had died. And there is the stone of unction, on which the body was annointed; another, on which the angel sat who anounced Him risen.

In a small chapel, of white marble, perpetually lighted by gold and silver lamps, is an empty sarcophagus; revered for ages, and by half the world, as the sepulchre of Jesus. For fourteen hundred years, the palmers have dared all danger to print their lips upon its cold surface; and kneel beneath its artificial halo. For its possession the armies of two continents, the the chivalry of two religions, waged ferocious war for centuries. Around it yet, hereafter, perhaps at no far distant period, will surge and struggle the last great battle of the universe.

It is still the prime object of promiscuous curiosity and devotion. It is besides, the central point of those christian celebrations, which alone disturb the monotony of the city. No other town, in ordinary times, has so dull and dreary an aspect. There seems to be no absorbing business. There are none of the attractions and improvements of the day. It has no magnificent monuments or palaces; no architectural piles like Paris; no museums of art like Rome; no colossal remains like Thebes; no signs of enterprise like London. You do not hear the hum of spindles, the clank of hammers, nor the roar of furnace fires. No vast establishments are burthened with crates. No drays distribute merchandise; no railways rattle with trains; no electric wires flash intelligence.

The gloom of night is uncheered by the light of gas; and the tedium of the day is unbroken by the arrival of a regular mail, by the issue of a newspaper, or the sight of coach or wagon. There are no juries, no learning, no eloquence in the courts; and neither skill nor science amongst the sick. There are no places of amusement, no theatres, nor promenades—nothing of modern style or spirit. The mass are practically ignorant of all the progress of the last century. And though imaginative, they are without philosophers, scholars, artists and politicians.

Traffic is limited to the sale of relics, beads, and holy water. The inhabitants live on the credulity of pilgrims. The streets are narrow, dusty, crooked, filthy, steep; some with steps like stairs; some closed up like courts; nearly all darkened by overhanging stories, and mats stretched across for shade; and many filled with heaps of carrion and rubbish.

Yet these thoroughfares are the places of chief resort. There trade bargains; faith prays; justice flogs; medicine prescribes; poverty begs; aristocracy sips coffee and smokes; the barber cleans pipes and shaves heads. There sits the merchant, cross-legged, on his calico, waiting for a bid, but contented without one. There the baker, her brow adorned with coins, holds up, between her tatooed fingers, bread baked on heated jars. There passes the Bedouin, bristling with weapons, and breathing disdain of towns.

You see there the huge camel, with his freight of bales, and stomach like a bath-tub; and the lunatic, raving, as his neighbors think, with inspiration, muttering nonsense, which passes for prophecy; and the physician, commanding almost as much reverence as the madman, while he does not know the difference between the lungs and the liver, and though in a livery red as blood, is ignorant of the circulation of that fluid in the body. And the Pasha, with his ferocious sickle sword, his horse covered with rich housings, and two servants at the stirrups, with his pipe and snuff box.

There stops one to pick up a scrap of paper, lest, perhaps, the name of Allah written on it, should be trampled down, and desecrated. You see the beggar asking alms, and receiving it, or is gently promised it to-morrow—for the Moslem deals kindly with the poor. You see a crowd of wolfish dogs, whom no one owns, and every one feeds. And the police officer restoring peace with his thong of rhinoceros skin.

You see the judge, who smokes while he condemns the murderer to a fine of one hundred camels. And the schoolboys, who complete their education by learning, in a singing concert, to read the Koran, and to count a hundred on their fingers. And the scribe, with his inkhorn in his sash, such as Ezekiel saw, writing from right to left, on his hand, as on a table.

You see the Moslem funeral train, moving to the grave already full, with rapid step, for the soul they say, is restless till the uncoffined corpse is buried; while hired female mourners beat their bosoms, tear their hair, and cry in their artificial anguish: "He was here yesterday, he is gone to day, he will not return to-morrow." You see the bride going to her husband's home, escorted by a bevy of companions with splendid dresses and wretched music.

Every Moslem has a right to four wives, though he often waives it on the score of economy and quiet. Divorces may be had for asking, but the offspring, and her portion follow the mother. Parties are betrothed, without a personal acquaintance, by their parents. Thus the burthen of courtship, and the torture of suspense are avoided; love is postponed till the marriage; and the torch of Hymen lights the arrows of Cupid. Young brides often tease their husbands by visits to their kinsfolks, in order to heighten their ardor by absence, and prolong the novelty of the honey moon.

They live apart in the harem; where they gossip, quarrel and embroider. But they can neither read nor write, nor sing a line of music. They do not mingle with the other sex at parties, prayers, or meals. They are never the subject of conversation amongst men—it would be as indecent to remark on one's faults, as to inquire about the health of his wives. Generally their close or partial mask of muslin, like the silver veil of Mokanna, conceals an ugly face. Their brilliant eyes are exposed, and flash with magnetic sparks—the true telegraph of passion.

They ride out on gay donkeys, seated astride, with a boy behind to goad the beast, and direct its course. They walk about in yellow slippers, muffled up in sheets like corpses, and seen amongst the graves which they visit on Fridays, look like the risen ghosts of the cemetery. They are regarded as toys, at times as slaves; their salvation is a trifle, as they are superseded in Paradise by women made of musk.

The dwellings are chiefly stone; with flat roofs for sleep or rest; dark in the basement; the door lock is a bolt, and the door key a nail driven in a stick. The second floor is terraced, furnished with mats, divans and ottomans; and windows are long and latticed, to keep out both sun and sin. Proverbs are pasted on the walls, as talismans against vermin, but with apparent ill success. Amulets are worn as bracelets to guard against unlucky days, and the evil eye.

They eat on the floor; use napkins for plates; their fingers instead of knives and forks, and thus enjoy at once both touch and taste. They are forbidden the use of wine, but stolen waters are sweet, and stolen liquor is sweeter; and men get very drunk on arrack, distilled from dates.

You see them in the bath, where, after passing the ordeal of heat, steam and soapsuds, a servant rubs off the skin like shavings; cuts the nails to the quick; places them on a couch; and there, inhaling smoke through rosewater, and sipping coffee thick as honey, from cups like egg shells, they anticipate the ease, the aroma, and the beverage of heaven.

You see the story teller, enchanting crowds with a beautiful mythology of Peris and Fairies; with the gallantries of angels; the exploits of dreadful robbers; the merits of sainted Sheiks; reciting fables about jeweled halls; groves with silver leaves; women fair as the blossoms of jasmine; warriors firm as rocks; horses swift as the storm; hospitality generous as the dew; fidelity true as the stars. You see also the exhibition of the various rites of the true faith and the false.

Such is the present condition—such the stupor, the superstition, the ignorance of this city, once so populous and polished.

She was once favored. The Deity loved her better than all the dwellings of Jacob. She was esteemed as the type of the first paradise on earth, or of the last in heaven; carrying the mind back to the Eden of

Adam, and forward to the new Jerusalem of the Apocalypse.

She was once the fairest city beneath the sun. On her ivory throne sat the wisest of terrestrial kings. In her gorgeous temple, dwelt the Lord of Hosts. All around and within, were sights of unequaled beauty. The golden walls harmonized with the wealth of nature. The lofty spires, brilliant as alabaster, matched the voluptuous fertility of the soil. The rippling brooks answered to the singing birds. The flowers of the valleys vied with the precious ores of the mountains. Fair fruit hung upon the trees; and the vines bowed with their delicious burthens. The cattle pastured on a thousand hills. The fields waved with continual harvests. Groves breathed odoriferous smells. The presses flowed with oil and wine. The music of cymbals was heard in the dwellings. Silver was like stones in the streets. The heights of Lebanon furnished her with cedars. The Sidonian artists were her cunning workmen. Syrian merchants supplied her with purple. Egypt sent her horses and linen. The mines of Ophir poured gold into her coffers. The ships of Tarshish wafted her cargoes of silk and ivory. Monarchs went thither, like pilgrims and subjects, with presents and tribute. And from the river to the land of the Philistines, and the borders of Africa, there was none who did not do her homage. Secure and happy, she had no rival, and she feared no foe. Peace was within her walls, prosperity within her palaces, and she was the marvel and joy of the world. History, with all her volumes, has no other page like hers. Nor has imagination, with all her poetic colors, painted a fairer picture. The fables of the golden age, the tales of romance, scarcely surpass the authentic glories of the Jewish city.

But behold her now! How changed, how sad she seems upon her desolate mountain, shorn of her charms! Widowed, wailing, and in sack cloth! Despoiled, and trodden down; without a chief, and without an altar! Her childen scattered like the wind strown leaves! The signs and the prophets have failed her, and her God is deaf to her prayer!

But still she hopes, still looks for the promise, when her wanderers, from all the lands, whither they have been driven, shall return with arts, knowledge and treasure. When her waste places shall sing, and her walls be laid with precious stones. When she shall be called to rise from the dust in her beautiful garments, and be throned again in her pride.

THE EASTER FESTIVAL.

Pilgrims annually resort to the Holy City, in order to celebrate the Easter festival, in the church which covers Calvary. On the first day of the feast, the Greeks, with many tedious ceremonies, buried the Saviour. The next morning, the Latins performed the Invention of the cross. On the third day, when the fire is believed, by the people, to fall from heaven, there ensued a sight which beggars all description.

A vast multitude, various in costume, complexion, and dialect had come together—from the hills of Attica—from the villages of Abyssynia—from beyond Jordan—from the coast of Barbary—from the shores of the Baltic—from the banks of the Bosphorus—from the islands of the Mediterranean. They poured into the church like a tide at the flood. They crowded every avenue, gallery, and niche,

> "All access was thronged;
> The gates and porches, but chief the spacious hall
> Thick swarmed."

Murmurs rose from them like the moaning winds of the mountain pines. They swayed to and fro, with anxiety and impatience. A procession of Greek priests, with symbolical banners, and the Patriarch at their head gorgeously robed, struggled around, and then stopped, before the tomb. The latter entered, and at length a torch, feigned to be miraculously fired, was handed from the holy shrine. Thousands of candles were instantly lighted. Faces, hands, and bosoms were bathed in the flames, deemed sacred. The excitement grew intense, and became phrensy. The tumult waxed louder and louder. They yelled—they howled—they prayed—they cursed—they screamed. They flung up their arms—they leaped on one another's shoulders—they rushed against one another in opposite currents—they fought like furious beasts. The police rushed amongst them with thongs and scourges, striking in all directions. It seemed if all were engaged in one promiscuous battle. Every violent, every wicked passion was let loose. Clothes were torn into rags—limbs were broken—dangerous wounds inflicted—faces disfigured—and life was lost.

This fearful scene continued amidst noise, and smoke, and heat, till dusk. It seemed more infernal than human; more like a revel of fiends, than a feast of Christians; more fit for any other spot than around the supposed sepulchre of the Saviour. The Catholics and Armenians, however, long ago, denounced a ceremony so disgraceful, and even the Greeks are said to be growing ashamed of its scandal and impiety.

The next morning afterwards, the numerous devotees were seen, thronging through the different gates of the city; on foot, on mules, in great companies, and in pairs, departing for their far off homes, amidst the contempt of dogs and Turks. So terminated that feast, which was once so popular and important in all the christian Church; which cost so much labor and discussion to fix the period of its return; which occasioned rules in councils, decretals, and the new Calendar; which was intended to commemorate the Resurrection; which corresponds with the passover of the Jews; which is called after that Pagan mistress of the passions,

> "To whose bright image, nightly by the moon,
> Sidonian virgins paid their vows and songs."

JORDAN ROBBERS.

I employed a sheik and four men, the usual guard for this journey. But the dragoman considering himself and the sheik sufficient for protection, sent his men and the baggage to meet us at Jericho. Well mounted, we passed eastwardly over desolate hills of stone and sand, down ravines, along the edge of rocks, and in six or eight hours we reached the spacious plain of the Dead Sea.

A strange loneliness and gloom prevailed. A few bushes were seen, but no birds were there, and a single gazelle was the only creature that crossed our path. The mountains of Moab cast doleful shadows upon the mysterious lake. Its heavy waves rolling slowly upon the beach, rattled like sheets of metal, or like muffled bells, the requiem of the buried cities. I bathed in its waters, transparent as glass, and which buoyed the body up, and burned the lips like vitriol. The blasted shores seemed strewed with salt and brimstone. The atmosphere was impregnated with a bituminous odor.

We proceeded up by the shores of the Jordan. The sheik and dragoman were in high spirits. They displayed their skill in the saddle, and the mettle of their horses. They galloped forward, returned, and grasped objects on the ground without stopping. The sheik had a long lance, the only weapon in the party, and charged with it on imaginary foes. Both careened wildly around, shouting and laughing defiance at all the Bedouins in the land.

We halted at the spot on the Jordan where they say the Saviour was baptized by John. I was smarting from my asphaltic bath, which seemed to have robed me with a shirt of fire. I sought along the borders of that narrow and tumultuous stream, for a place to wash in its lucid waves. Disappointed by the abrupt and crumbling banks, I was returning, when some twenty armed Arabs came stealing towards us from the bushes. For an instant it seemed they might be friends. But their numbers, and movements, showed their hostile purpose. They were as wild and picturesque banditti as ever robbed or killed. They crouched like beasts of prey, or like hunters, or like Indians, with their pieces leveled. They advanced behind the sheik and dragoman, as they were watering the horses. I shouted the alarm. My men rushed into the stream. Unseen before, I became the target of a score of guns. A bullet whistled near.

I took shelter behind a wild fig tree, whose branches reached to the ground. There quite helpless, without even a penknife, stick, or stone for defence; suspicious of my guides; ignorant of the language, and of the country, I had to await the issue. The imagination was not inactive. Stories of highwaymen and savages, of barbarian slaves and tortured captives, passed swiftly through the mind. For a time, the chance of escape appeared hopeless.

Four Arabs, with guns and knives, prowled around the place I left, and within the shadow of the tree which sheltered me. Some of them stood off on guard to prevent surprise. Some searched the saddle bags. The others secured the horses; dragged the guides out of the water, and stript them to their shirts. Part of them mounting our beasts, they all went off in triumph and swiftly disappeared.

From necessity we walked over rocks and sand for several miles, and entered Jericho very tired and very humble. There my men, like David's messengers, were compelled to tarry for breeches, though not for beards. Having rested and refreshed, I proposed the next morning to the Turkish officer, in command there of ten soldiers, a joint expedition, at my expense, against the robbers. He laughed at the scheme, and said it was impossible to find them in the mountains. Then observing that I had escaped without the loss of clothes or money, he added, very gravely, that "Allah had already blessed me."

A trifling number of Arab huts compose the modern village of Jericho. Some foundation walls, and crushed aqueducts, are all that remain of the ancient city of palms. From its elevated site, a wide and sorrowful prospect stretches over the once populous and prosperous plain. You may see whence went up, as from a furnace, the smoke of the guilty cities, for which Abram pleaded with the angels, and which ten righteous would have saved. You may see where Zoar stood, which Lot entered as the sun rose, when forewarned, he escaped for his life. You see Pisgah, where Moses beheld the land he should not reach—where Israel crossed dry shod the Jordan, and kept the first passover in Canaan; and threw the ancient walls down by the trumpets and the shouting. You may taste of the spring Elisha sweetened, and pass by the house of Zaccheus.

Hence to Jerusalem the way leads over high hills—by public wells and fallen Khans—along rough paths—through suspicious places. Some one of which, was the scene of that parable, which showed who was neighbor to him that fell among the thieves. Thence on by Bethany, by the house and tomb of Lazarus, where Mary met the Saviour, when his tears told how he loved her brother.

THE JEWS.

The Jews are a marvelous people. They have retained their individuality, their sabbaths, their ceremonies, through all the vicissitudes of thirty-five hundred years, and in all the regions of the globe. Other races have flourished and left splendid monuments of civilization, and been lost amongst the crowds of new generations.

We cannot to-day recognize the descendants of those who built the mysterious temples of Thebes; nor of those who enjoyed the palaces of Nineveh, and the hanging gardens of Babylon; nor of those who raised the columns of the Parthenon; nor of those who shared in the glory of the Forum, and the triumph of the legions. But the Jews are among us now, claiming a national character, which throws in the shade the oldest dynasties of Europe.

It existed when the Druids sacrificed at Stonehenge; when barbarians, in wolf skins, hunted on the banks of the Seine; when the Assyrians worshiped in the temple of Belus; and the Pharaohs reigned in the valley of Egypt; before the Cæsars ruled Rome, or the Orators ruled Athens. They have suffered for ages. They have been persecuted, branded, banished, enslaved, sold like cattle, tortured, imprisoned, cursed, cropped, stoned, crucified, torn by wild beasts, put to the sword, committed to the flames. They have been vagrants on the earth, the byeword of the nations, seeking peace, but obtaining none—

> "Like that bird of Thrace,
> Whose pinions find no resting place."

Yet as serfs, nobles, felons, outcasts, bankers, beggars, and martyrs, they have always been a peculiar people, clinging to their traditions, standing ever on their ancient ways.

As a nation, they were not distinguished in the arts and sciences. Their prophets were poets, and soared to the "highest heaven of invention." Their historians were graphic and concise. But they made little progress in mathematics, in astronomy, in chemistry, in painting, in statuary, or in architecture. They no more contrived their house of worship, than they formed their laws. The Temple, like the Pentateuch, was a revelation. It was a type they could not improve, and durst not copy. Nor was divine knowledge exclusively confined to them. It had been experienced by the Gentiles before the Exodus, and between that period and the Christian era.

There were some wholesome doctrines in the creed of the old Orientals. There was the perfect and upright man of Uz—the believing priest of Midian—the righteous king of Salem—the devout Centurion of Caesarea—the resolute faith of Socrates—the sublime sentiments of Plato—the beautiful pastoral of Virgil. But these were single instances, or obscured by grossest errors, and only glimpses of the truth. While the word was given to Israel with the die of heaven on it.

Their leaders spoke face to face, with the Deity, as with a friend. It was their dwellings which the angel of death passed over. It was their camp before which went the pillars of cloud and fire. For them the floods stood upright, and the sea became dry ground. For them the sky rained manna—the rocks gushed with water—the fruitful land was conquered. Yet they forgot this miraculous care. They followed after strange idolatries, heathen abominations,

> "And oft forsook
> Their living strength, and unfrequented left
> His righteous altars; bowing lowly down
> To bestial gods."

They sacrificed on the eminent places, in the valleys, under the green oaks, to license, homicide and hate. They stoned the prophets, sent to warn them of sin and judgment. They crucified Him who brought them a new covenant—who taught them a new commandment—who would have gathered them under his wing.

The day of visitation came upon the Jew. How low he stands amongst the tombs of his fathers, and in the very city of his soul. Jerusalem, in Hebrew, the inheritance of repose, yields none to him. Even there he finds none more humble than himself. He beholds the symbols of fanaticism over the place whence the daily sacrifice ascended with the sun. He hears the imposter's cry—"There is no God but God, and Mahomet is his prophet," from the spot where the priest was wont to say—"The Lord bless thee and keep thee."

All around him rise associations dear to his heart—the lessons of childhood—the words of the law—the anthem of the singers—the visions of promise. The voices of ages ring in his ears. The spirits of the past crowd before him—the faithful—the prudent—the mighty men of old—heroic leaders—lofty prophets—illustrious kings. He recalls the faith of Abraham, the sagacity of Moses, the inspirations of Esaias, the mourning of Jeremy, the victories of David, the glory of Solomon. He sighs for the departed sceptre. He weeps more bitterly than the captive Daughters, when he remembers Zion. Burning, but not perishing; blinded by obduracy; infatuated with his exhausted Ritual—he denies the miracle he proves—he still fails to comprehend the truth and clemency of heaven—he still fails to perceive the light which shone through the parted Vail, and whose risen brightness is illuminating all the nations but his own.

BETHLEHEM.

This renowned place is a village of about two thousand people, and is situated on a ridge of rocks. The streets are like bridle paths, but they are sufficiently convenient, as there are no wheeled vehicles in all the land. Beads, made of wood and berries, shells rudely carved with scriptural scenes, and asphaltum cut in the shape of bibles, are the staple articles of traffic. Women are seen in gaily colored shawls, such perhaps as the Virgin wore; and such as Raphael has painted in the Madonna della Seggiola.

A large church and convent, of different periods of construction, cover the supposed place of the Nativity. A kind of cavern, such as in the East may be sometimes seen, occupied as stables, is in one end of the building. The natural roof is concealed by drapery. A star on the marble floor marks the birth place of the Saviour, and a silver plate on a polished altar, indicates the site of the manger. Some score and a half of costly lamps are there burning, night and day. Pilgrims, from all quarters, are continually meeting in this subterranean chapel, and pressing their lips upon the consecrated stones.

Near by, is the room in which St. Jerome wrote the Vulgate scripture; and adjoining it, are the graves of Eusebius, of Paula, and the innocents, slain by Herod.

From an eminence may be seen a valley, circular as a basin, and the only fertile feature in the landscape. There, they say, the startled shepherds heard the angels' voices, "announcing peace on earth and good will to man." In an opposite direction are the three pools of Solomon. They are ranged one above another, they once supplied Jerusalem with water, and still seem large and full enough to float a fleet. Towards the north, a small plain building, with a dome, its walls scribbled over with letters of all languages, is said to be the tomb of Rachel.

These localities may not be the sites of those events with which tradition has identified them. But in this neighborhood those marvelous scenes occurred. Hither Joseph and the Virgin came to be numbered, and taxed under the edict of Cæsar. Near here, stood the crowded inn; the stable, in which the son of man was born and cradled, over which shone the auspicious glory of the star; and in which the rejoicing Magi poured out their bales of precious gifts.

This was also the scene of David's youth. Amongst those hills and glens he kept his flocks, and grew in comeliness and vigor. Here he was anointed by the prophet; and his character moulded by that grace of heaven, which inspired his victorious heroism over the wild beasts and the vaunting giants—his tender friendship, passing the love of woman, which knit his soul with Jonathan's—his exalted patriotism, in relieving the beseiged Keilah, when its ruler sought his life—his generous forbearance towards the helpless, hostile Saul—his strict justice, in slaying the sons of Rimmon, the murderers of his foe—his lofty continence towards the beautiful Abigail—his noble self-denial, in refusing to slake his thirst in water, procured by the periled life of friends—his magnanimous confidence in the hospitality of Achish, his enemy—his patient dignity, in enduring the curses of the son of Gera—his affectionate grief over the loss of unfilial Absalom—his judicious and compassionate policy towards the conquered rebels—his sincere repentance for his crimes, and unfaltering faith under chastisement—his prolific genius, chanting praises and prophecies, in strains immortal.

RELIGIOUS SECTS IN JERUSALEM.

Various religious creeds are represented in this city. It seems like a capital of catholic worship—the shrine of all believers. You see the observance of three Sabbaths in one week; adverse ceremonies in the same chnrch; hostile pilgrims bending over the same tomb.

The Imaum in a green turban, the badge of Mahomet's kindred, explains, on holy Friday, the faith of Islam. The disciple must wash his hands and feet in sand or water, as a wholesome preparation for meals and worship—curb his appetite by fasting, and on certain days abstain from even the odor of a flower—abhor idols, avoid blood and swine, any thing strangled, accidentally killed or naturally dead. He must make a pilgrimage to Mecca; with his face thitherward, pray five times a day, by standing, kneeling and prostration; and remember that the oftener his brow meets the ground, the greater its proof against infernal fires. He must believe in inexorable fate; in the unity of God; the mission of the Prophet; the existence of Genii, liable to be damned and capable of heaven. He must watch for the signs—the issuing of a monster from the Kaaba, the advent of Jesus, the appearance of Gog and Magog. Then the filling of the earth with smoke, the speaking of dumb beasts, and a strong wind which shall sweep away the faithless. Then the opening of the judgment when each one's words shall be weighed, the crossing of the narrow bridge to Paradise, the draught at the Prophet's pond. Then the repose beneath that tree which satisfies all desires; whose shadow reaches over a journey of a hundred years; from which flow streams of wine and honey; by which lovely virgins dwell, with all the charms of sense, and all the purity of spirit, not made of clay, but perfumes.

You meet the Greek priest, who wears a black velvet robe and square cap, and represents the largest branch of the Christian Church. He believes in transubstantiation; predestination; the invocation of saints; the propriety of pictures; the efficacy of relics; the immersion of infants, and their communion on bread sopped in warm wine and water. But he rejects instrumental music in the service; the doctrines of infallibility, supererogation, and indulgences.

The Franciscan monk mortifies the flesh, in a coarse brown robe, girt with a cord. It is his only garment, and he wears it night and day.

The Copts are the scribes, and write for the government, and for the ignorant. They may be seen in white turbans, with puffed cheeks and mulatto skins, scribbling from right to left in the police office, or at the street corners. They believe in one unmixed nature of Christ, in transubstantiation, circumcision, and the baptism by fire.

The Armenians are the merchants, the farmers of customs, the shippers, and traders by caravans. They may be seen in their gaudy and costly church, whose walls are lined with porcelain, partaking of the communion as they lie prostrate, amidst the ringing of bells and the glare of torches.

You meet the Pilgrim with the white dust of travel on his sandals, borne thither many a league, to see the blessed city of three religions. He comes to bathe his shroud and body in the Jordan, holier than Abana or Pharpar—to loiter amongst the avenues and fountains, and bend in worship beneath the lofty dome of Omar's Mosque. To behold the scenes, hallowed by His incarnation, whose life was truth; whose miracles were charities; whose passions were virtues; who mingled the attributes of two natures; the graces and glories of two worlds; the authority of a spirit, with the humility of a mortal; who sealed his humanity by death, his divinity by resurrection.

You meet some of those descendants on whom their fathers invoked the retribution of His blood. Who are strangers there as elsewhere; a few of them in affluence, but secluded; many of them sustained by foreign alms.

FROM BEER TO TYRE.

Beer, the Mickmash of the scriptures, which gave Jotham a refuge when he fled from Abimelech, is now a squalid place, filled with dogs and children, who bark and howl at christian trowsers when they pass. Beyond, the road is rough, toilsome and perilous, and leads by streams and gaps—through villages of mud and stone. You meet women with tatooed cheeks and chins, carrying pitchers on their shoulders, recalling the days of Rebecca. You see mounted Arabs, of sinister aspect, arrayed in flowing blouses, with long spears, journeying like errant knights, or the highwaymen of the novels. You see a camp of Pilgrims, returning baptized from the Jordan, with mules and horses decked with jingling bells and Bethlehem beads.

You pass the field which Jacob purchased when he came from Padan Aram; and the well he digged. There, long after, the Saviour wearied with his travel through Judea, met the woman of Samaria, and taught her of that water, which springs up unto everlasting life; and of that devotion, which prefers to worship, neither on the mountain, nor in the city, but in spirit and in truth. You see where Joseph was buried when brought out of Egypt; and the rude monument which the Moslems have raised to him, as one of the Patriarchs of the Koran.

On opposite sides are the lofty mountains of Gerizim and Ebal, where the people heard the blessing and the curse.

Near by, amongst olive and orange trees, with birds singing, and water purling through the streets, is Nablous, once Shechem, a name as old as Abram. There, the remnant of Samaritans dwell, retain their ancient faith; sacrifice four times a year on the top of Gerizim; and chant their service on Saturday, their Sabbath. You may listen before the church, which none may enter except barefooted or in slippers, and an officiating clerk with others, will leave the altar and beg you for a present.

Half a day beyond, on a high point, in view of the sea, a deep valley around it like a vast moat, is the site of ancient Samaria. Two Arab huts, a ruined church of the middle ages, built, it is said, where the Baptist was beheaded, some marble columns in rows, prostrate and standing amongst growing corn, occupy at present the capital seat of the idolatrous kings of Israel, and the ten lost tribes. Jezreel is now Jezreen, a village of fifty souls, where Naboth was murdered for his vineyard, and Jezebel eaten by the dogs. From its elevated situation, with little Hermon on the right, and Mount Carmel on the distant shore, you may look over the magnificent valley of Esdraleon, the battle field of Napoleon, and of Saul; and Shunem, where lived the widow whose hospitality obtained the blessing of the man of God.

Nain is still the name of a village, where that merciful miracle restored her only son to the widowed mother, as she went weeping after him to the grave. Half an hour beyond, on a wild and cavernous hill side, is Endor. Calves are stabled, and hens nestle in the grotto, where the Witch, at the troubled king's entreaty, disquieted the rest of Samuel.

Passing by Mount Tabor, which rises, like a perfect cone, glorious amongst the mountains; and over some undulating ground, covered with live oaks and lentil bushes, you descend with the evening shadows into the vale of Nazareth. The town of white houses is beautiful at a distance, but foul within. The spot where Gabriel hailed the virgin; the shop, a cave, in which Joseph wrought; the rock on which the Master and his disciples ate, are amongst the traditionary localities of the city, in which Jesus passed his youth. Cana of Galilee, is now a christian village, and associated with the miracle which made the water wine.

Beyond the mountains, covered with wild barley, where the multitude feasted on the loaves and fishes, and left fragments, is Tiberias. Its walls are rent and shattered as the earthquake left them thirty years ago. There is the sea on which the disciples toiled with their nets; on which Christ walked; whose waves he stilled in the storm; from whose shores he spoke in parables to the people.

The great Mount Hermon is on the left, crowned with snow. Opposite are Bethsaida and Capernaum, those stubborn cities, the scenes of mighty works which would have saved Sodom from her fate. A day's journey thence is Acre, famous for the siege and failure of Napoleon. Within the vast area of the plain around it, armies might have room to battle for the empire of the world. Passing thence along the coast, you meet, perhaps, a Bedouin driving a dromedary and a pair of kids, as presents for some marriage feast.

Traversing a tongue of land which extends far into the sea, you enter over piles of dirt, an humble village, whose streets are small, and foul as sewers. You see men and boys fishing from the foundation rocks of ancient castles; and the only ship in the harbor, receiving a cargo of excavated monuments! This is Tyre! The blasted witness of her own sins. She has accomplished her predicted doom. She exhibits, to-day, the desolation which the Seer beheld, when she was the glorious city of the sea—when the nations traded in her fairs—when commerce sailed in her navies—when her palaces were gorgeous with golden dust, and stones of fire!

PASSPORTS, CUSTOM HOUSES AND QUARANTINE.

Every traveler has had cause to complain of these three institutions. He is apt to believe that they were intended to obstruct international intercourse. The time which they cause him to loose; the irritation and imposition to which they expose him; the fees and bribes which they compel him to pay, are sufficient reasons for his prejudice. That he must carry with him, in time of peace, an official description of his person and citizenship, to show that he is not a revolutionist; that he must consent to the invasion of his baggage, to convince petty officers that he is no smuggler; that he must be deprived for days of his liberty, in order to prove that he has no infectious disease—are regulations which do seem to militate against the spirit of the times.

Some of these inconveniencies are much modified by the liberality of governments, and the politeness of its officers. Yet no delicacy in its administration can make the passport system very popular. That document requires the seals of the police office of the place one leaves, of his own national representative, and of the representatives of the countries through which he will pass, and to which he is bound. As the offices at which applications must be made, for this purpose, are open only at certain hours; are often a considerable distance apart; and often thronged; serious delays consequently occur.

Being desirous of hastening to Italy, I was obliged to await three days the official permission for the journey. Before I could leave Genoa, it cost me three or four dollars for the necessary vises. Though a servant can usually procure the proper signatures, yet in Rome I was compelled to go several times, myself, to the public department, and barely escaped being arrested for somebody else.

One's passport is often taken from him at the gate of a city, and only returned when he is ready to depart, as in Vienna. Sometimes it is sent to his destination in advance, as from Boulogne to Paris. In Alexandria one is furnished with a new one in Arabic, to suit the prejudice of Mahometans. It is important to carry it, in other instances, about the person, for it may be demanded anywhere, day or night, and the inability to produce it would be a cause of detention. Any defect in it, is a source of trouble; a fellow passenger was sent back for miles, on that account to Strasburg. It is the occasion of continual expense; is taxed by every one who touches it; and costs about twenty dollars a year. It is, however, a ticket of admission to certain museums, and remains afterwards a curious record of one's route.

Custom Houses are not inconsistent with good government, but the practice of searching private property is always offensive. Some officers merely go through the forms of an inspection, open the lid of one's trunk, and close it. Some faithfully derange every parcel;

unfold the packed linen; probe the empty legs of boots; and open the leaves of a journal. One replied to an objection against a rigorous search, that he had found jewelry in stockings; that boots were now and then filled with tobacco; and books with lace. But a small coin will universally induce the subordinates to assume, and assert the contrary.

At Liverpool, a quarter of a dollar, surreptitiously given, stopped the inquisitive hand of the clerk. A fine segar removed the suspicions of the German agent in Austria. While in Italy, and the East, bribes were openly demanded, and at times reduced by chaffering. An odd incident occurred to myself, and four others, who went from Rome to Naples, by veturrino carriage. By this agreeable arrangement, the proprietor of the conveyance, for about $4 a day, for each person, provided the accommodations. All of which, the candles, the fire, the items of the meals, the style of lodging, and the "*buona mano*," or presents, were specified in the written contract.

We passed over the Appian way; its large pentagonal stones, here and there preserved; its borders lined with brick and marble ruins of tombs and arches, aqueducts, and temples. We passed the supposed spot where Coriolanus yielded to his mother's prayer for Rome; where Clodius was slain by Milo; where Ascanius was buried; where Pompey had a villa; by a lake said to cover an extinct volcano, and then into the town of Albano; and lunched in the former palace of Charles the fourth of Spain.

Thence by Aricia, where Horace lodged when he went to meet Mecænas, situated on a hill, walled and dirty, where women in red jackets and blue skirts were sitting at a well, or carrying water on their heads in copper jars. We slept at Velletri, where Augustus was born; whose streets are steep, and whose houses of stone are like stables, both in odor and construction.

Thence through the Pontine marshes; between double rows of elms; over a well paved causeway, without curve, or hill, or toll gate; with meadow and swamp on either side; the haunts of plovers, snipes and thrushes, of brigands and wild boars; and dined at the Forum Appii, mentioned in Paul and Horace.

Thence by men in black pointed felt hats, and breeches of rags, or skins; by donkeys tottering under heaps of hay or wood, near "the goodly city" of ancient Antium, where the Apollo Belvidere was discovered. Then near that promontory where Circe had her palace, and her prison for the comrades of Ulysses. Then to Terracina, hanging on a rock two hundred feet high, the sea roaring at its base, and the last city of the Pope's.

On reaching the Neapolitan frontiers, as the spokesman of the party, I was invited into a room up stairs. There the collector, exhibiting great affability, instantly gave me, to present at the next office, a certificate that our baggage had been properly examined Surprised at his liberality, I cordially and innocently tendered him, after the Italian fashion, a thousand thanks, and deferentially bowed out of his presence backwards. A shade of disappointment, however, seemed to cross his face.

Seated in the carriage, I astonished my companions, by describing the graciousness of the agent; and while we were all concluding that his government was better than its reputation, a soldier came to the window, and claimed pay for the certificate. We incontinently laughed outright at this proof of our own blunder, and his impudence. One of our number offered him a huge copper *bajocco*, bearing the image of Garibaldi, once worth about three cents. He shrugged his shoulders, and naively declined the currency, which just then represented an obsolete idea. As we drove off he leaped on the box, with the driver, determined to convince us that his superior ought to have been bribed.

At the next office, we showed our clearance, but the person in charge having conversed with the soldier, disregarded it. Rather than be stopped, with five large trunks, whose examination might be maliciously prolonged, we offered him five francs. He refused them contemptuously, and demanded an exorbitant sum. The porter, by his orders, began to unload the luggage. I followed him into his room, where several were seated around a basin of hot coals, and mildly expostulated; spoke of our urgent haste; and broadly alluded to a letter, which I had to the Pope's chamberlain. Leaving the driver with him, I returned disappointed, to our party.

While they were indulging in a little audible profanity, the officer came up to me, hat in hand; regretted the misunderstanding; commanded the trunks to be strapped up again; saluted us with a "good voyage," and remained with his assistants, uncovered, till we were out of sight.

This extraordinary turn to our fortune, was soon explained by the driver, to have been due to his ingenious lying. On his own motion, taking the hint from the letter spoken of; he represented that I was an American ambassador, and the others my suite. Though properly vexed at this deception, it was gratifying to know that the government had not been slandered, and that its extortioners had been defeated. This, however, was the only instance of such luck, which fell to my lot; the rest of my experience was generally expensive and unpleasant.

Yet neither custom houses nor passports are as intolerable as the lazaretto, for it includes the evils of both, and adds to them personal restraint. As it is always located at the termination of a weary route, by sea or land, one does not enter it with much enthusiasm. The uneasy saddle of the camel, and the restless deck of a ship, are preferable to a prison.

My first quarantine was performed in the suburbs of the scriptural town of Gaza. The building was large, rectangular, with small cells, whose windows and doors faced an open court in the centre. The closing of the heavy gates on us excited a sense of oppression, and a regret that Samson was dead, and a habeas corpus would not lie in the bailiwick of the Philistines.

After an exposure of five days to a Syrian sun, blazing within the walls, as in a tube, and to those vermin referred to in Exodus; after panting in an atmosphere which had no chance of circulation; and lodging in apartments for which a grand jury would indict a jailer; feeding on sickly indigenous chickens, served on iron dishes, by a waiter who used his shirt sleeve for a dish cloth, and the tureen for a wash basin —we were glad to accomplish our legal purification, and like an exhausted congress, to be allowed to go "without day."

Some months afterwards, we repeated, with some difference, the same ordeal at Smyrna. The table was unexpectedly good, fish and figs being conspicuous. The crowd was so great that several were lodged in one room. I was thus compelled, every night, to hear a discussion between a French count and a Socialist, whom the quarantine, like misery, had made bedfellows. The chattering of pet monkeys; the cries of infants; the yelping of curs; and the wailing songs of Orientals, also helped to disturb one's temper and repose. The charges imposed were nevertheless unconscionable; but our release made us generous, and we paid them without murmurs.

On the coast of the pretty island of Syra, I entered a lazaretto for the last time. The rooms were large and high; the wild sea dashed its waves against the walls below, and famous shores were in sight around us. The fare was vile; the meat tough or tainted; the bread "dry as the remainder biscuit after a long voyage." The waiter was old, deaf, decrepit and blear-eyed; the cook regarded neither cleanliness nor godliness. To all our remonstrances, the incorrigible stewart replied by apologies—to every delinquency by a promise of repentance—his politeness increased with our indignation. He disarmed the curses of one, by giving him the appellation of Effendi; and the assault of another, by saluting him with the title of Pasha. While he thus saved himself by "soft answers," like a christian, we had to be hungry and submit.

18

The company, various and social, contrived notwithstanding to be amused. There, among others, was a Greek, whose rich language still rings with historic accents—a German, with his objective and subjective dogmas—an East India Englishman, fluent with brilliant narrative—and Symriote women, eloquent with love and beauty. Thus parties—flirtations—dances—concerts—the soft airs of passion—the heroic hymns of nations, made some amends for the hardships of durance and diet.

CONSTANTINOPLE.

This is Constantinople!—here, at the confluence of two seas—by the contiguous shores of continents—with its panorama of spires, and masts, of trees, and cupolas, and the Golden Horn!

Skirted by a wall of brick and stone, crumbling like the empire, with cannon on the quays, is the Seraglio. Its palaces have marble rooms for bathing, and long saloons with latticed windows, and matted floors. Groves of evergreen and sycamore adorn the grounds. Its Porte, or gate, gave name to the government, and under its arch, ambassadors formerly waited an hour beneath an uplifted axe. The numerous widows of the late Sultan, are imprisoned in one of the mansions, according to custom, for their lives.

Behind it, is Saint Sophia's—once a church, now a mosque—which, it was said, an angel planned; and at which, an Emperor toiled. It is of grand dimensions, and rich materials; and to it, every quarry seems to have contributed stone, and every temple columns. It is furnished with little else than mats, and rugs, and pendant lamps. Its tapering minarets, and swelling dome are so light and graceful, that they seem floating in the air. Far back, rises the snowy summit of Mount Olympus. The tideless sea of Marmora mingles the color of its waves with the distant blue of the horizon.

And there is Tophane with its quay and fountain; Pera with its Franks and Dragomans; Galata with the fire tower, built by the Genoese.

The streets are only winding alleys, offensive and unclean. The houses appear to have been built downwards, their tops are so much larger than their bases.

The shops will not admit either the vendor or his customer. Hucksters are numerous, selling cherry water and fresh fruits. The carriages are gaudy as Christmas boxes, without springs, and the coachman walks. Jewish women have tires like crescents around their heads, such perhaps, as the prophet spake of. Porters carry saddles on their backs, and compete with the donkeys.

There are tombs of the Sultans, decorated with marble, with pearl and cashmere. The cemeteries occupy more ground perhaps, than the city. Some of them are places of promenade and pastime; where jugglers perform their tricks; bands of music play; well dressed people take refreshments; and the constant odor of death pervades the air. The Hippodrome with its obelisks; the Burnt Column; the Brazen Pillars with serpents' heads; two of the Seven Towers, and The thousand and one columns, under ground, the resort of bats and ropemakers; are some of the relics of the ancient City of the Emperors.

The existence of a fire is made known by a light on the tower, and by the discharge of guns. The firemen and water carriers, run with water skins and hooks and axes. The engine is borne on the shoulders of two men; mounted policemen, and the Pasha direct the operations. The Dancing Dervishes, a sect of Mahometan monks, perform their devotions on Tuesdays. An old man, all in green, bows towards the East. The others, in tall white felt hats, and white robes, squat on the floor. A slow nasal chant is commenced by one, and at the tap of a drum, all fall flat upon their faces; rise instantly to their feet; and march round a circle, in measured time.

Soon they throw aside their robes; and in white jackets and sort of petticoats, revolve by the hour, with the regularity of spindles; while the oldest passes through them; stamping his foot, to increase their enthusiasm and rapidity.

The Turkish women wear thin white veils, and appear to be homely, pale and freckled. The men have abandoned turbans for Fez caps; and many wear the Frank costume altogether. We crossed over to the other Continent, and climbed the steep and toilsome heights of Bulgurlu, to enjoy its enchanting prospect. We wandered through the cemetery of Scutari, with its evergreens waving over the once turbaned tombstones, and the costly sepulchre of Mahmoud's horse.

Here was an exhibition of the Howling Dervishes. Having either embraced the Sheik, or kissed his finger, ring or turban; all sat on the floor in a circle, and commenced a low prayer. Then standing up they began a guttural chant, and swayed their bodies backward and forward. As they elevated their voices, they increased the velocity of their motions. Growing excited, they redoubled their exertions, until their concert became a frightful howl; most of them fell exhausted, trembling, and foaming at the mouth, like maniacs. The Sheik during the ceremony stood on the breast of a child to cure its sickness by a miracle.

We went up the Bosphorus, whose name recalls the story of Io—on whose banks the retreating Xenophon reposed—through whose swimming rocks Jason adventured for the Golden Fleece. Its indented shores inclose many placid lakes—are enriched with luxurious summer palaces—with vales fairer than the meadows of Damascus—with waters sweeter than the wells of Paradise—with villages shaded by the pendant branches of fig and mulberry—with monuments to heroes—with fallen altars to the gods.

Such are some of the attractions and features of the Sultan's city. Nature has not formed, nor man selected, a grander site. It seems fitted for the capital of universal empire. No wonder that it has been so long a tempting prize—that it has been the battle ground of races and religions—that it is still the paramount object of international jealousy and ambition.

THE SULTAN, ABDUL MEDJID.

Crossing the bridge of boats, which join Galata and Stamboul, I was startled by the sudden thunder of artillery, announcing the Sultan with a fleet of steamers, returning from a tour. As he came up the Bosphorus, the sea and city trembled with the boisterous welcome of a thousand cannons. The flags were flaunted from the masts, and towers. The quays were crowded with the people. The shopmen forsook their stalls. The beggars left their haunts. The cripples forgot their lameness. The women, in their curiosity, pushed aside their veils.

When night came—the illuminated windows; the fireworks blazing amongst the cypress trees; the lamps shining along the ropes and port holes of the vessels; and the sounds of pleasant music, prolonged the joy and lustre of the day. While this reception showed the popularity of Abdul Medjid, scarcely any one obtained a glimpse of his person.

On the next Friday, the Moslem sabbath, I engaged a caique; one of those delicate boats, light as shells, which, sharp at both ends, skim the water like a sea bird. Seated carefully on the bottom, to preserve its balance, with the oarsman dressed in white trowsers and embroidered shirt, we hovered about the mouth of the Golden Horn, to see what mosque the Sultan would that day visit. It was in the warm month of June, and the scene was such as no other spot can display.

At last the signal gun was fired, as the Sultan left the pier of his Asiatic palace. He was attended by four large caiques, one in advance, and two others in the rear of the one he occupied. Seen in the distance, the long procession—moving in a line—swift as an arrow—glistening in the sun—seemed like a train of light upon the wave.

The drawn bridge was covered with the bayonets of soldiers as he entered the Golden Horn. In the most magnificent of the barges; which appeared to be a combination of a gondola and a canoe; with painted sides and gilded prow; manned by twenty-six seamen, whose burnished oars kept a measured beat upon the waters; sheltered by a canopy of silk on golden pillars; seated on a cashmere cushion; with his officers at his feet, and their faces towards him—sat the Monarch of the East.

He passed on, leaving behind the flapping sails, the curling smoke of steamers, the shoals of small caiques, gliding like playthings on the current. Amidst the roar of guns from towers and navy; the flashing of flags; and the loud swell of martial music, he landed at Eyoub—opposite which his predecessor launched the ships that won the city.

He walked for some distance on a carpet, spread out for him; through a passage lined with veiled women, and wide trowsered men. He then mounted a white horse, richly, but not gaudily caparisoned, and rode slowly to the sacred mosque, in which the sovereigns are inaugurated with the sword.

The crowd treated him with becoming respect. There was no marked sentiment of awe. They gave a peculiar salute with their hands. But they made neither genuflexions nor prostrations. They did not manifest any enthusiasm. The men gave no cheers—the women waved no handkerchiefs. Not a murmur of approbation was heard. But they regarded him with some pride. They showed uneasiness at the presence of foreigners, and expressed indignation when they approached near his person.

He was a young man, of the ordinary height, and of a slender figure. He wore a Fez cap, a red woolen cylindrical article without a rim, adorned with a jeweled tassel on the crown. He had on a dark frock coat, fastened with cords of braid, and white pantaloons. His mouth was concealed by a moustache. His face was brown and pensive. You could read there no trace of great emotions; no ambitious dreams; no consciousness of power; no fear of responsibility. It seemed impressed with the fatuity of his religion; with the gravity of his race; and with the mildness of his life.

One could hardly realize that he had a hundred wives; that he reigned over the fairest region of the world; over the eastern half of the Roman possessions, from the cataracts of the Nile to the shores of the Euxine, and from the Bosphorus to the Adriatic. That he would risk a war, perhaps a throne, in order to discharge the duties of hospitality to Kossuth. That his army would win battles in a conflict with Russia. That he himself was described as the shadow of God.

He seemed more like the sick man of the Emperor Nicholas. With a debilitated frame, and a hopeless constitution, he was a type of his declining empire. His subjects are enervated by idleness, tobacco and polygamy. They are said to be honest, but not so conscientious, as formerly, against wine and usury. There is one newspaper devoted, they say, to anecdotes about the sagacity of animals. The schools produce few scholars. The courts may be said to be without juries, and without advocates. Commerce is in the hands of strangers. Religion promises a sensual paradise. Women are uneducated. Soldiers are influenced by fatalism, as likely to inspire cowardice as courage.

The Sultan has, therefore, no intrinsic resources for the continuance of his power. He relies for political existence, not on his navy, which Americans built; nor on his army, which Frenchmen disciplined; but on foreign troops. He expects actual aid, when necessary, from those nations who filled the ranks of the Crusaders. The successor of Saladin is sustained by the successors of the lion-hearted Richard and Philip Augustus; and the Crescent floats under the shadow of the Cross.

ATHENS.

Sunset was flinging gay colors over the heights of Paros, whence were obtained the blocks of the "Medicean Venus," and the "Dying Gladiator," as we left the pleasant island of Syra. The next morning we reached Athens,

"A place *we* longed to see, nor car*ed* to leave."

The city has a picturesque situation, amongst historic seas, isles and mountains. Battles, earthquakes, and two thousand years have marred her monuments, and quenched her altars. But her rivulets, plains and ruins have peculiar charms. The halo of ancient days still sheds a beauty on the scene. One may fancy the shades of the past still lingering near—that he hears eloquence murmuring in the winds; reads poetry written on the leaves; sees art mirrored in the waters; and valor springing from the ground. Every thing has such classic features; nature wears such a heroic aspect, that you cannot deem this a common soil, nor the mother of common men. It is marked by the footsteps of great souls; and every sense proclaims it a land of glory.

Look all around—scarcely any other prospect is so full of interest. Every view is associated with some famous incident, or some grand idea—with some achievement of the hand, or intellect, which has influenced society for centuries.

Standing on the top of Pentelicus, whose quarries are yet open, which furnished the marble of the ancient structures—you may see on one side, the crescent shore and green plain, with its tumulus of soldiers; and on the other, the distant bay with its rock bound walls; recalling the victories of Miltiades and Themistocles, and the immortal names of Salamis and Marathon. Climbing the Acropolis, greatly elevated above the sea, and insulated from the other heights, the scene of the fabled spring of Neptune and olive of Minerva; and you are before the Parthenon.

It was the temple of the Citadel; associating an erroneous faith with public security, it was a splendid expression of the national taste and superstition. It is in ruins; its cella shattered; many columns prostrate; the ivory image of the Goddess gone; the elaborate frieze of Phidias disfigured and despoiled; yet it is always the world's great model of architectural beauty and proportion.

Near by is the Pnyx, now as of old, an open hill side, with the Bema, the pulpit rock of eloquence, shaped like an altar, facing the mountains. It was there, the orators roused and ruled the murmuring masses; and shook the distant thrones. Yonder flows the Cephissus, now driving a mill wheel; now irrigating a garden; now wandering through the olive groves of Academus, once animated by the discourses and the school of Plato.

There, is the Doric fane and tomb of Theseus, beautifully preserved; a memorial of posthumous gratitude over the ashes of the hero; while around its portico the

Peripatetics listened to the teachings of the Stagirite. There, in the solid rock, is the prison cave of Socrates, reminding us of his life—almost christian in its virtues—and of his death, which excited the repentance of his judges, and drew retribution on his foes.

On the left is the Stadium, of immense capacity, scooped out like a valley or the basin of a lake, from whose inclining sides, now overgrown with grass, the populace witnessed the contest of the races. There, two columns remain of the theatre of Bacchus, once trod by buskined actors in the tragedies of Euripides; and resonant with the shouts of the multitude, when Demosthenes was crowned with gold.

And there, most memorable of all, with solid stairs and stools of stone, is the hill of Mars. It was the seat of that renowned tribunal, which met at night to insure justice, against fear and favor. It was there, before Areopagites, Stoics and Epicureans—before the news-seeking citizens and strangers—and the magnificent display of idolatrous altars—some mocked, and some believed, the apostle of the Gentiles, when he stood in their midst; setting forth a strange doctrine of resurrection and judgment; a new religion of faith and repentance; and the Unknown God, who dwelleth not in temples made with hands.

There, scantily supplied by the fountain of Callirhoe, trickles the almost waterless Ilissus, on whose banks the Lyceum flourished. Beyond, rises the ridge of Mount Hymettus, now bright and fragrant with the blossoms of wild thyme; and swarming, as ever, with myriads of honey bees. On a vast artificial platform, tower the colossal relics of Jupiter's Corinthian temple.

It was begun under a domestic tyrant; finished by a foreign conqueror; and the progress of its construction kept pace with all the eras of democratic rule.

These are some of the wrecks and localities of this early, brilliant republic. She declined, and with her gods and heroes passed away. Spoiled by success; betrayed by corruption—she sowed the seeds of her dissolution, by ingratitude to her best citizens. She appreciated their worth, when it was too late, when they were in exile, and in the grave; and like another nation, the sons garnished the tombs of those, whom the fathers stoned.

Turning from these reminiscences, you may, in the moonlight evenings, on the public walks, mingle with the modern Greeks. They wear gilded jackets, white kilts, and crimson caps. They have brilliant eyes; flowing hair; a most musical language; figures and faces like ancient models; a fondness for liberty and novelty; and a natural quickness of intellect. They have little business enterprise; some men of learning; a respectable bar; an ignorant clergy; and a reputation for veracity, unfortunate, if only half deserved.

Their monarchy of constitutional limitations recognises universal suffrage, and virtually destroys it, by official interference at the polls. Their revenue hardly pays the labor, or the avarice of those employed in its collection. The interest of their public debt is discharged by those who guarantied the loan. Their navy of one ship, and army of ten thousand men, are more for the security of the rulers than the people.

Their King is an alien by birth; dresses in the native costume; speaks imperfectly the language; amiable and diligent, but incapable; and surrounded and controlled by mercenary parasites, and foreign agents. The royal palace, which vies with the richest in Europe, was built on the ground of an Englishman, who was paid through the intervention of the British fleet. Such is Athens, poor without paupers, independent without power; but her history, and her monuments will make her a place of pilgrimage for ever.

LETTERS OF CREDIT.

Travelers usually carry a special letter of credit to some particular house; or a general one, in printed form, addressed to the bankers of various cities, who endorse on it the sums they respectively pay. And although one loses something by commissions on these payments, he avoids the trouble of transporting coin; and is able to draw the amount he requires, in the currency of the place in which he stops.

With a letter of the former description in my pocket, I boarded a steamboat, bound on an excursion around the pleasant Isle of Wight, whose circumference is some sixty miles. It was a summer day; but the wanton wind leaping from the sea, and the fresh spray spreading rainbows above us, made the atmosphere delightful. The music of adventitious harps and organs, and the shifting panorama of the shore, excited and amused the crowded decks. The insular circuit was soon made—the castles; the towns; the deep caverns; the tall chalky cliffs, called the Needles, rising from the sea like the spars of an iceberg; the river and the streams; the distant Osborne palace; the white sand banks, used in making glass; the arable acres mantling with their harvest grain, or animated with the pasturing flocks; were at length all passed, and we landed where we started, and dispersed.

Sauntering from the wharf, I missed my letter as I entered the hotel. It was a quiet tavern, peculiarly English; such as Shenstone lauded for its welcome—promising clean linen and roast beef; with a tidy young woman to make out the bills; and a head waiter for host, whose apparel, of white and black, was a cross between a cook's and a parson's. They showed a proper concern for the loss of the letter, and suggested a reward for it. That evening, the ancient streets of Ryde were disturbed by the clatter of the bellman, who, with all the zeal of Dr. Syntax, in pursuit of the picturesque; or of Diognes, with a lantern, seeking an honest man, endeavored to discover the thief, or finder, by an offer of compensation. But nothing

> "Was found
> By the crier in his round
> Through the town."

Although the letter could not have been used without forgery, I concluded to prevent any chance of its payment. I took the first conveyance to Portsmouth, and in an express train, through Brighton, sped like a missile to Folkestone. Thence over the channel, rough enough to disgust all landsmen, to Boulogne; famous for that failure of Napoleon, which history proves was the shadow of success. Urged through the vociferous mob, of blouses and moustaches; my passport and baggage, sent for examination to the offices; two meals "rounded with a sleep;" then seated in one of the cars, which, like the English, are divided in compartments, sufficient to contain eight or ten persons; we were borne swiftly to the gay capital of France,

The vast depot was furnished with counters and clerks, who, presuming every one to be a huckster, searched the trunks for produce, subject to market duty. My inventory having satisfied the official, I inquired of him how I could immediately find Mr. G. With many graceful gesticulations and apologies, he regretted his inability to answer. Perplexed, like the Oriental, who was bound in a limited time, to find a stranger in Bagdad, I was about yielding to defeat; when the railroad superintendent directed me to the establishment. I was there relieved of further anxiety.

I never heard of the missing note. Some repentant rascal, perhaps, may reveal its story on his death bed. It may have drifted down amongst the subterranean currents, and torn, worn, in fragments, or in powder, made the circuit of the seas. It may have gone into the everlasting limbo of lost things, with the lost arts, the lost books, and the lost tribes. Six months afterwards, however, calling, by chance, at the post-office in Rome, I unexpectedly received one in lieu of it.

The fate of a similar letter occasioned a serious disadvantage. On going to Egypt I informed the banker that my address after certain named dates, would be respectively at Cairo, Beyrout, Smyrna, Constantinople, &c. With this understanding, I was disappointed on my return down the Nile, in not receiving a remittance at Cairo. I wrote about it to various places in vain. The dust, the fleas, the flies, the heat, the approaching summer, made that city less attractive every day. After a long delay, I met, accidently, an American acquaintance, who supplied me with a sum which would be temporarily sufficient, if I could get cashed the order I obtained in Rome. The German banker repeatedly evaded my application; but fearing that it would be soon unsafe to cross the desert, I enlisted the interest of the Vice-Consul, Mr. Kahill. Our united courtesies at last subdued his brusqueness and compunctions.

Eight weeks afterwards, while moving along, poor in purse and spirit, I saw with delight the fig trees and oleanders of Beyrout. Before shaking off the dust of travel, I inquired at the banker's, only to be told that he had nothing for me. Our Consul, Mr. J. Chasseaud, however, on reading an introductory note from Mr. Cass, Jr., obliged me with the required money.

I reached Smyrna, supposed to have been built by Tantalus; and where my disappointment recalled his punishment. When the minarets of the Eastern capital hove in view, it seemed impossible that I could be longer embarrassed. Yet here I learned that such a letter had been sent to Smyrna; that the steamer was injured; and her mail, by some error, had been forwarded to Beyrout.

A month in Constantinople exhausted my curiosity and resources. With a cordial introduction, under a printed heading, and stamped with the official seal from a public functionary, to a member of our Embassy, who was then in the United States; I expended my last guinea in a journey up the Bosphorus to visit his substitute. He received me well; perused the letter with satisfaction, and invited me to dine with him. But as he replied to my financial narrative, by scratching his organ of cautiousness; and an abrupt reference to Eastern antiquities, I declined with forced politeness to eat his salt. That night the countless dogs of the city seemed to be barking at my misfortunes.

But in the morning a Scotch traveling acquaintance, to whom I related my diplomatic experience, voluntarily replenished my exchequer. Having repaid the Consul by a draft; and arrived at Athens; instead of money, I received notice that funds would be sent to Venice. This was a fair prospect, but of no immediate importance to hotel keepers, and steamboat captains. The Caledonian again opened his purse.

Venice, I do remember; not only for its beauty and uniqueness, but also, because there, after a fortnight's patience, came the long desired heavy envelope. No commission was ever more grateful to the weary office hunter; no bauble was ever dearer to longing child; nor love missive to pining maid, than that small parcel was to me. I returned to the good Scotchman, just as he was leaving the city, his loan, which only that morning he offered to increase. This letter explained the mystery about the other. The first had been mailed in England, but the postage not having been prepaid, it lay a week or more in the office. It was then sent to Constantinople, and reached there before I did, and thence as already stated.

One year from its date, while in the University of Berlin, the lost letter came, defaced with many inscriptions and printed marks, and taxed five dollars for postage. During the same year, on the Alameda of Seville, "famous for oranges and women," I was pleasantly surprised to meet the generous Scot. Again, after an interval of a few months, when in Paris I gladly reciprocated his favors, when he was also disappointed in a remittance. Such annoyances as these had their compensation; for they protracted a sojourn in places of interest; elicited the confidence of strangers; and gave rise to lasting attachments.

> "Florence! beneath the sun,
> Of cities, fairest one."—*Shelley.*

As the stranger enters a cafe, in Florence, a pretty girl, in a large leghorn hat, will probably give him a boquet. This, however, is only an appeal to his silver, through the medium of a sentiment. He is expected to pay for the courtesy.

Yet the place is attractive to both the economical and the curious. Wine and books, galleries and landscapes, fleas, garlic, and fine weather, are abundant. Invalids, artists, authors, and people fond of mediæval associations, make it their residence. No tourist will neglect to visit this beautiful city of St. John.

If public celebrations please him—he may, perhaps, witness the races of Roman chariots; or youth, with paper lanterns, rejoicing around the festooned altars; or the imposing procession of robed dignitaries, following a golden Christ beneath a pall, while the bells toll, and the monks chant for "the dead of all time."

If he is familiar with the genesis of curves—he may study the structure of one of the bridges, whose use was prohibited, while the nature of its arches was discussed.

If he would see paintings—there is the ideal beauty of the Virgin, which Raphael's pencil has incarnadined.

If he would see sculpture—there are the "intoxicating charms" of the unveiled Venus; and "the thought of Michael Angelo" in the marble face of the sitting Lorenzo.

If he would see groups in bronze—there are the gorgeous gates in the Baptistery, which admirers have deemed worthy of Paradise.

If he would see precious stones—he may enter cabinets, sparkling with the water of a mine of gems; or that unrivaled Medicean chapel, designed to shed its lustre on the Saviour's tomb.

If he would see architecture—let him trace the delicate lines of Brunelleschi's dome, as they swell upward in elegant harmony with the great vault above them.

If he would see libraries—there are halls teeming with manuscripts and volumes, oriental, and classic.

If he would enjoy gardens—he may saunter by grottos and by statues, along arched and open alleys, brilliant and fragrant with unnumbered plants.

If he would have prospects—he may gaze from the Cyclopean walls of the ancient Fiesole, on a scene which once charmed the unclouded sight of Milton.

If he would go where they have laid their historic dead—he will find the genius of all the arts doing homage at their shrines.

If he would know the eventful progress of the city—he may read on her pavements, in the aisles of her palaces and churches, how she caught up the torch of knowledge from the sepulchre of nations; and echoed the eloquence of democracy in her piazza, when the Pnyx was no longer known at Athens, and the Comitia had disappeared from Rome.

Long she flourished in opulence and influence. Her armies, her bards, her artists, her statesmen, and her merchants filled all countries with her fame.

She became enervated. She yielded to the silver yoke of splendid tyrants. She was a slave.

There she stood for centuries; leaning on her ornaments; her delicious hands in fetters; her melodious lips sealed; her radiant eyes turned sadly toward the past; fixed, silent, and cold, like the marble Greek of Powers. But still beautiful!—still exquisite in her pensive trance!—waiting for the spark of freedom to quicken her spirit, and kindle her graces to their appropriate splendor.

AGRICULTURAL ADDRESS—1855.

It is not the purpose of this discourse to give lessons in farming. Such matters as require study and experience I was not asked to discuss, and do not presume to teach.

"Non tam procul absim ab Urbe."

My humbler task is but to diversify the entertainment of the hour, and give some, though inadequate expression to thoughts which the occasion universally inspires. An appropriate topic is this exhibition of earth's bounty, and man's enterprise, suggesting whatever is pleasant in the annals of industry, the marvels of nature, or the promises of time.

What assurances of plenty, what pledges of progress, does this promiscuous scene afford! Its success manifests the public partiality towards a most important interest. It is a wise policy which periodically concentrates in one place all that is beautiful, and strong, and wholesome; which covers the ground with contributions and spectators; with fair ladies, fast horses, fat oxen, tall corn, stout men, shanghai chickens, and monstrous melons; with huge machines, which cut ten acres of grass in a day, and thresh eight bushels of wheat in an hour; with churns, which always bring the butter; rakes which revolve, instead of breaking; drills which sow better than the hand; ploughs which do not choke, and run almost alone in the furrow; harrows which crush the clods like millstones, and substances which make the barren places smile.

Thus, to bring together the best varieties of every department, and have their qualities, their culture, and all their appliances examined and explained; to have their defects exposed, and their merits tried; to have the criticism and judgment of the crowd upon them, is surely a wholesale method of imparting and obtaining information.

Innumerable examples also prove that such public displays promote no less their immediate object, than the harmony and instruction of the people.

Other exhibitions, aided by the swell of music and glare of tinsel, have allured men to grosser scenes—in which wrestlers strove; or boxers parried; or gladiators fought; or bacchanalians rioted in drunken festivals; or errant knights sought in the perilous shock of lances the love of ladies; or steeds were gored by Spanish bulls; or painted players shocked by their contortions, or disgusted by their folly.

But this—unstained by violence or blood; with no act of shame or horror, to raise a blush or draw a tear—spreads forth a spectacle as picturesque as peaceful; teeming with the charms of beauty, intelligence and taste; with every thing which tempts the appetite; excites the gentle emotions, and kindles the fancy. Where the banquet, the graces and the flowers combine. Where agricultural ambition finds a proper impulse, and ingenuity the recompense of reward; where intercourse extends the sympathies, chastens the manners, improves the sense. Where observation gathers facts, and suggests invention; where local prejudices are worn away, party animosities assuaged, and impositions exploded.

County pride may gaze here with complacency on the spoils of her bosom; and even patriotism may be gratified by a display, which bears pregnant proof of a noble land, and equal laws. Encourage then, these annual shows, which, like the world's great Crystal palaces, exhibit the triumphs of industry, the treasures of the year, and the advancement of the people.

But such spectacles as this have the peculiar attraction of the open country. We are away from the noisy streets, and the red walls—

"*Un*cribbed, *un*cabined, *un*confined—"

Where no floor supports, and no roof shelters—amongst the sources of what we celebrate—enjoying the sweet breath, the fair charms, and the pure oracles of nature.

Where else could we pursue that magnificent theology which expresses itself in the panorama of the universe; in the ever present miracle of life and growth, and dissolution; in the ever changing kaleidoscope of the seasons; in the grand diapason of earth's ceaseless music.

Here, every object is an altar to faith, and an inspiration to genius. Here, the pure affections have their dearest exercise, and the superior faculties their most exhilarating themes. Here, misfortune may obtain a refuge; weariness, repose; and sorrow, a healing balm; the weeping eye be cheered with visions; the broken heart with soothing voices. Here, youth learns the first lesson of humility; old age the last of resignation; scepticism repudiates the divinity of chance; passions subside; and virtues flourish.

Here, are the subjects of art and science—the geologist delves amongst the strata; the shepherd watches the stars; poetry holds up the magic mirror; philosophy reads the open volume; true eloquence learns its rhetoric; painting its outlines and colors; music its voluptuous tones; architecture its principles of construction, and sculpture its materials and models.

"God made the country, man made the town."

The Deity loves to "dwell in temples not built with hands." On the lofty summit of his footstool he proclaimed the written law. It was in a garden, that as a friend, He walked with our frail parents. And the Son in whom the Father is, taught most, along the waysides of Galilee, on the coast of lake Tiberias, and on the mount of Olives, the resurrection and the life to come—while the landscape answered like an echo the wisdom of the teacher.

Man finds an elevating sense of freedom in the open air. The soul feels unfettered, when no walls surround and no ceiling covers—devotions seem to rise to the very gates of heaven—the thoughts expand as if the world attended—the imagination wanders forth, exulting like an angel.

Thus ancient error often constructed his idol altars, and burned his sacrificial victims on the hill tops; and left his temples without roofs. So justice was administered at the outer gateway of eastern palaces. The famous Areopagites sat uncovered on the hill of Mars. The populace heard their orators, and framed decrees in the face of the Ægean winds. The Sophists taught and disputed, as they strolled through the groves. The historian and the bard contended for the laurel on the plains of Elis. In the unsheltered Forum were once made the laws of Rome.

Thus natural scenery is associated with the great drama of the world, and the records of the race. And towards it still, the human disposition, however occupied, fondly turns for occasional refreshment, or ultimate enjoyment.

The citizen oppressed by the unwholesome air of sultry streets, hastens to the rural districts. The lover, "sighing like a furnace," or weeping like a shower, haunts the beech trees to carve his immedicable wounds and melancholy passion. The parson seeks the exercise and recreation of the farm, to restore a frame wasted by the zeal of his vigils and his weary load of cares. And the physician, tired of arduous duties and thankless errands through the cold, the darkness and the tempest. And the mechanic, whose cunning and industrious hand has spent its force on works of usefulness and taste. And the merchant, fatigued with the busy commerce which unites the nations, and the jarring interests and perplexing games and ceaseless noises of the market. And the lawyer, sick of selfish struggles, uncertain issues, and human frailty obscuring truth and foiling justice. And the sailor, shattered by the hardships of the ocean, and the storms that howled their hoarse Æolian strains through the vessel's rigging. And the statesman, whose single genius saves the welfare of the state, and nobly wins, but never wears the laurel on his brows. And the soldier, forsaking his sanguinary honors; and the magistrate, his dictatorial powers, resort at last to the simple labors of the plough.

What avocation then, shall be compared to his, which brings him in continual communion with the works of nature? Who, through the day and through the year, goes forth with the sun; toils with its hours, and slumbers with the shadows. Whose senses are pleased by such an endless variety of beauty? Whose labor gives more salutary vigor to the frame, or better feelings to the heart? Whose arm wins noble trophies in the game of trade, of office, or of battle? Whose soul has sweeter contemplations in the visions of the morning, or the dreams of night? Whose life has a fairer mission than the subjugation of the soil, attended with the blessings of contentment and independence, the facilities of knowledge, and the persuasions of religion?

An occupation so attractive is also the oldest and most universal. Before society was formed, or kingdoms rose, or tribes assembled; before the fisher angled, or the hunter trapped; before the ground was cursed, it was farmed. God's first commandment was to dress the garden.

The first of human toil was tillage, as it may be last. Coeval with the race, it spread and descended through all countries and all ages. Sometimes dormant, but not entirely lost even amongst the savage hordes, it ever has been, and must be forever, the great business of the world. No less the support of individual life than social vigor, it has built the cities and organized the nations.

Then cultivate the bounteous earth; make the fields glisten with the whitening harvest; fill high the granaries with corn—and behold! how the public welfare prospers! Victory follows, like a slave, the invincible valor of your armies. Your navies sweep resistless over all the oceans; your commerce flaps her white wings in every harbor; trade fills the towns with the music of a million wheels; your senate speaks with the voice of oracles; grateful incense smokes upon your altars; happiness smiles upon your hearths, and glory, like a halo, covers all the blessed land.

History wherever it has written, tradition wherever it has spoken, show what agriculture has accomplished, and how it has been honored. It has been the care of great rulers, and the theme of gifted bards. The oldest people of the East, and the strongest people of the West made laws to foster and protect it. It is, to-day, a study in European universities. It inspired "the works and days" of Hesiod, and the Georgics of Virgil. Mago, the general of commercial Carthage, and Cato, the censor of the Romans, wrote of it in many books.

Ceres and Osiris were once worshiped as its deities. But the ancient farmers, in their erring piety, paid homage to a lower order of divinities. Every stage of the sprout, every grass of the field, every leaf in the forest, every stream in the vale, every sign in the Zodiac, were peopled by inferior powers. Not a bud bursted, nor a fruit ripened, nor a grain took root, nor a water drop fell, nor a sunbeam warmed, nor a color gleamed, nor an odor exhaled, nor a zephyr blew, nor a particle of soil was enriched, nor an animal was born, without the care and permission of its peculiar god. The plantation was a rural pantheon. Invocations mingled with the daily task; and festivals, with dancing and with shouting, closed the labors of the field.

We have corrected the theology, but may not have excelled the crops of those who farmed the plains of Mantua; or the cattle which grazed near the Sabine hills; or the flocks of the Arcadian shepherds; or the horses of the Epirian shores.

Thousands of years ago, they burned the stubble, sowed, harrowed, destroyed the tares, and raised their stock nearly as we do now. They improved the quality of grains; acclimated foreign seeds; accelerated or retarded germination by cropping the branches or boring the bark; compounded different growths; knew those whose affinities cause them to fade or flourish when near together, as the rose becomes sweeter by the garlic; dwarfed, and altered the appearance, color and produce of various plants.

But we have surpassed all before us, in lightening the duties of the season, by transferring to machines the drudgery of labor; in discovering new fertilizing substances, and easy means for their transportation; and in scientific knowledge of the soil. And all these advantages have been realized in the present century.

Fifty years ago, these neighboring grounds could hardly support their tenants. The herds were driven over distant tracts for pasture; the grain fields were vast, but poor. But the introduction of cloverseed, of lime, and other agents, doubled and trebled the productions of the soil.

Old implements, and old customs have been superseded. The long wooden plough, the wooden harrow, the sickle and the flail, are disappearing fast. The reapers are not often seen, in animated contest, gathering the grain in their bosoms. The sound of lusty threshers is rarely noticed beating time upon the hardened ground. The huskers' jolly party, of men and damsels, are no more heard singing by the moonlight, as they strip the yellow corn. The apple paring matches, and the quilters' pleasant frolics, have ceased to cheer the big old fire place with the jovial airs of the fiddle, and the fantastic footsteps of the jig. The hand looms have become almost peculiar to the prison; and the spinning wheel is seldom whirling its industrious round. Few flax pullers ply now their merry task. The water smeller, with his hazel twig, is no longer called to locate the draw well. Not many now regard the sign that sinks or soars, when they lay the worm, or thatch the hay rick.

Gone are the days of the cocked hat, the buckled small clothes, the ruffled wristbands, and the fair topt boots.

But women, as odd as amiable, have, by their basques, hoops and high heeled slippers, connected those quaint old times with this stirring age of patent washers and elliptic springs.

But while fashion is capricious, useful enterprise has rapidly made an onward march. Nature has yielded revelations. She is not now the riddle and monster which past ignorance painted her; not now inscrutable, fearful, and, like the Sphinx with cruel lures, distracting all intruders. Science, like Œdipus, has invaded her dominions and despoiled her of mystery and terror.

But the conquest is unfinished. The future doubtless teems with untold blessings. We are but on the threshold of that region of invention, which shall open to us a new paradise; renew the original glories of the earth; disclose scenes transcending the voluptuous descriptions of the poetic age of gold, and as brilliant and ineffable, as the holy seers beheld in their prophetic trances. Such an era is consistent with the philosophy of civilization, and the logic of progress.

But a long and diligent probation must precede its advent. Education and morals must advance hand in hand. Inquiry and experiment must find new combinations of mechanical powers, new chemical affinities, and new classifications of natural facts. We must extend still further the range of the faculties and the senses; concentrate still more the conveniences and attractions of life; and give to each locality, generation, and individual, the advantages of all.

The spirit of improvement which has accomplished so much for other pursuits, must be directed more immediately to that which embraces and sustains them all. That we may supersede still more muscular labor; relieve still more the human hand; dispense with the servitude of bond and free; apply to the fields all the influences which facilitate intercourse, and the operations of the factories and shops; and perfect the organization of a class of workers, more potent and patient, more servile and systematic than men or brutes.

There is ample room and opportunity for ingenious effort. With a soil of considerable strength and richness, and a climate of average clemency, our agricultural appliances are but partially developed. Provision must be made for the contingencies of seasons, and the vicissitudes of weather. Something is required to save the crops from prevalent diseases. Something is needed better than tar about the roots for blight; or fumigation with sulphur, or whale soap wash, or steeping the grain in plaster, for insects; something better than lime water for mildew; or subsoiling for the drought; or raising from the seed to avoid the rot; and something to counteract the frost.

Machinery is insufficient. Some new power is wanted, less dangerous but as efficient as steam, to move the mower, the rake, the spreader, and the thresher; to drive the plough, the harrow and the drill combined; and something to husk the corn.

It is not improbable that some latent principle may yet be detected which will give an impulse and direction to husbandry it never had before. Which will take the place of every fertilizing agent known; obviate the necessity of alternating crops; condense the elements of growth, and make the germ ripen with electric speed—that the sower may one day scatter abroad, and the next day reap the harvest.

Or some process may be hereafter employed, which will make our acres yield in more abundance and greater variety, productions of which we have no example or conception; fruits, perhaps, sweeter than the peach; vegetables more excellent than the potato; grain better than wheat or corn. Our soil may yet supply us with the modified luxuries of those warmer countries, which have the genial influence of perennial summer; where the air is redolent with the blossoms of olive orchards, and shimmers with the Hesperian hue of orange groves; where the cotton, fig, and banana flourish.

Advances already made strip such speculations of extravagance. The arid desert, and the impassable marsh, have been made to bloom. The forest and the prairie have furnished our domestic animals, fruits and plants. Culture might still further increase the number of our gratifications. The persimmon, the gum, the service berry and the papaw might enrich the orchard; flowers still wild, would luxuriate in the garden; trees from the woods, planted by the roadsides, would vastly beautify the country.

Foreign esculents might be introduced with success. The yam of China for its pleasant flavor and nutritious properties; doura for its easy management and various uses; sorgho sucre for its forage; the bene plant for its medicinal oils. While the sunny slopes of a thousand of our hills offer their swelling bosoms to the generous vine. But start not at a vision of the Rosy God, reeling with his thyrsus beneath celestial liquor, and spreading about his steps the purple enemy of souls.

It is a true testimony, that wherever the vintage pours its blushing current—along the chalky hills of rich Champagne; from the tall cliffs and ruined castles of the fighting bishops of the Rheingau; from the old Moorish mountains of Granada; through the voluptuous Italian vales; from the classic islands of the Archipelago, and the holy places of "the morning land," you will scarcely see an inebriate from the use of wine. Yet the beverage is so common that it is used instead of tea or coffee, and drank at every meal; and so cheap, that beggars quaff it down like water.

In France alone there are one millions of acres of vineyards, producing one thousand million of gallons of wine in a year. It is only the cold northern nations, with whom the tender grape does not flourish, that are maddened by the fiercer distillations of the apple and the grain. It is they who sing the drinker's verse—

> "For baser tribes let rivers flow,
> Who know not *rum* or song,
> Man wants but little here below,
> But wants that little strong."

Whether or not the introduction of the wine press here would be judicious, is a question some future day may settle. And although in Ohio, the vineyards have yielded quadruple the profits from wheat, they have not yet found general favor with our husbandmen, who cultivate one hundred millions of acres, and whose annual productions reach sixteen hundred millions of dollars.

But on them—whatever the staples they prefer to raise; attached to the soil by interest and affection; supplying the granaries of the land; and keeping the very gates of the national wealth—a grave responsibility essentially reposes. With them is the last refuge of civil rights and social virtue. When agitation pervades the city, and men impelled by some pernicious passion, forget their loyalty to order; or when fanaticism kindles the fagot, or swings the gibbet; or foreign foes, or domestic treason, or corruption assail our institutions; when there is danger to the liberties, the laws, or the moral sentiment of the country, it is to the conservative force of the farmers we must look for hope and succor. Their unbending strength, and faithful patriotism must save the State from mischief; and uphold its wavering fortunes, as Hur and Aaron sustained the failing arm of Moses. Then

> "Ye generous *Saxons!* venerate the plough,
> And o'er your hills and long withdrawing vales,
> Let autumn spread his treasures to the sun,
> Luxuriant and unbounded.
> * * * * * * * *
> So with superior boon, may your rich soil,
> Exuberant, nature's better blessings pour,
> O'er every land, the naked nations clothe,
> And be the exhaustless granary of a world."

> Venedig liegt nur noch im Land der Traume,
> Und wirft nur Schatten heraus alten Tagen.—*Platen.*

Venice is built on islands, which are subdivided by canals, and reunited by a marvelous multitude of bridges. Foot paths and the sea touch nearly every door, and you may walk or sail all through the city.

The narrow winding streets are shaded by the massy walls of houses, and undisturbed by the noise and dust of horse or carriage. The shops glitter with Venetian glass and Oriental trinkets. The open squares have draw wells, and water carriers and print mongers—a handsome church, a curious museum, or a garden of plants.

But the magnificent piazza of St. Mark's concentrates nearly all the attractions of the place. It is an open area of several acres, paved with flag stones. It is partly surrounded by a covered corridor, which forms a brilliant arcade of stores and cafes, where merchants congregate, as they did once on the Rialto. On one side flows the Grand Cañal, in which large vessels lie at anchor; and numerous gondolas, those sable floating coaches, glide to and fro, driven by a single oar.

Here is the Doge's palace, and its audience hall, and council chamber, and library decorated with statues and gilded carvings—the Inquisitorial Apartment—the

Bridge of Sighs which the victim passed over to his doom—the deep, dark Dungeons of stone and iron, lined with oak and scribbled with dead men's names—the Great Staircase of the giants—the Red Pillars of the gibbet—and near by, the Pedestal on which the bankrupt was exposed to shame. Here are the trophy columns from Acre and Stamboul; and the three Masts, emblematic of the conquered kingdoms of the Republic.

Here is that remarkable cathedral of the patron Saint, built of rare materials, with an imposing array of spires, domes, arches and columns. It displays relievos from Persia and Palestine—bronze figures from the Archipelago—gates from St. Sophia's—spiral shafts of alabaster, which, they say, once stood in Solomon's temple. The facade and the interior blaze with mosaics on a ground of gold.

Here the flags fly on Sundays, and the cannon fires at sunset; and the band fills the air with music, as hundreds, few citizens, many strangers, stroll up and down amidst the glare of gas lights.

But for long years the city has not flourished. She had been the mistress of the seas. Founded by exiles, her position inspired her with independence and maritime enterprise. Many a famous feat and battle are written in her annals. She once ploughed all waves with her victorious keels. She carried her commerce and her cannon through the opulent East; stretched the sceptre of her Doges over distant isles; and filled her treasury with the tribute of vanquished states.

She was the seat of joy, and wealth, and art. She reveled in Carnivals, and Masquerades; she was a proverb for festivity. Her resources seemed exhaustless. All lands supplied her markets; Palladio planned her structures; Titian's pencil adorned her halls; Tasso's music floated on her waters. Her daughters were as queens, her merchants monarchs.

Her fortune was long propitious, her future fair. But she reached her political perihelion; her glory waned, and she was soon no longer known amongst the host of nations. And now she is no more free nor great; as much a subject as once a sovereign; stooping where she reigned; crushed as she once crushed others; suffering what she once inflicted; drinking the gall she gave her foes; brooding over prestige lost, trade declined, empty houses, deserted streets, grievous taxes, foreign soldiers, disastrous struggles.

But her history is fixed. Her name remains. Her palaces still stand. The Rialto spans the waters. The Winged Lion still spreads his pinions from the column. The Brazen Steeds are yet rampant on Saint Mark's. The Adriatic still offers her yielding bosom to the plighted Keel. Her rare scenery still endures.

And as we gaze on her various charms, we anticipate her better fortune. As the lingering lustre of the past plays around her horizon, we would fain believe the beams of her setting sun to be the gathering splendors of a new day.

GUIDES.

Guides in the old countries are often necessary to strangers, generally useful, and always expensive. Making allowance for the diversity of circumstances and temperaments, the tendency of their occupation gives them a uniformity of character, and one may be taken as a representative of the class.

He has usually a pocket full of papers, recommending him for qualities, in which he is apt to be deficient. His birth place is no part of the consideration of his engagement, but it is gratuitously referred to, as the locality in which he is expected to serve. His parents are often described, like those whose sons have their obituaries in the Newgate Calendar. His merits are hardly consistent, as the play-wrights say, with the probabilities.

He professes proficiency in the modern languages; and something like the preceptor in Juvenal, has the polyglot dictionary at the end of his nails. He is familiar with the geography of streets and museums, and marks out maps on his palms. He carries time-tables and hotel cards; has the acquaintance of the most reliable hackmen; has tried the most docile donkeys; and has sometimes a cousin who waits in the palace.

He has a knowledge of prices, distances, and contingencies. He knows where the best staples are to be had; where the condiments have the finest flavor; segars the rarest aroma; where the relics are genuine; and the amusements most inviting; where you can see the New York Herald and the London Times.

He knows what the man ought to have who makes the echo in Killarney; what is a sufficient *buona mano* to the Tuscan coachman; what is the conventional gratuity for passing pictures through the Custom House at Naples; what you must pay for a mummy's ring in Egypt; what is the discount on Austrian paper; and the premium on a pound sterling in Syrian piasters.

He knows by what gate the Emperor will leave the palace; when the Pasha is in the bath; when the fountains will play at St. Cloud; when the pilgrims will start for Mecca. He can tell how many may stand in the nose of the statue of Bavaria; how many steps to the top of St. Paul's. He names the officers on reviews; he points out the speakers in the chambers.

He is at no loss for explanations. He tells why the Irish round towers were built; why the women wear black silk on their heads in Malta; why they often wear but little else than veils in the East; how you can tell soup of horse shins by its redness; and the descendants of Mahomet by their green turbans. He points out where a child was found blinded by vermin, which were bandaged on its eyes, to make it an object of charity. He points out the mendicant, who begs on the Alameda, that his daughter, in silk and jewels, may ride on a mule; the government spies, who sit in the cafes; the Sheik robber, who is related to the Governor.

He has also been employed by men of note. He showed Washington Irving through the Alhambra. He was with the American expedition to the Dead Sea. He was with Lepsius when he lived amongst the reptiles and ruins of Karnak. He stood next to Louis Napoleon when he was special constable during the Chartist riots. He served Lamartine in Florence, and remembers that he commenced his studies before daylight.

He has always items of gossip. He says the Queen tore a button from her dress, and called Parliament a shabby set, for not appropriating more money for Prince Albert; that the Viceroy at Cairo makes no secret of drinking the blood of the grape, in defiance of the Koran; that the husband of the Spanish Queen is rather stupid, and of little importance, and that she herself is not as good as an angel; that the Duke of Baden compelled one of his courtiers to smoke some bad domestic segars, in order to encourage their manufacture; that King Otho's wife abhors England, and turned her back on English travelers as they passed her—and that his physician is so absent minded that he called one night on himself, and being told that he was out, slept at a hotel; that the late King of Prussia injured himself by "fast living;" that the late Abdul Medjid could not control the extravagance of his women; that in Munich, at her house with the gilded balcony, old King Louis visited Lola Montes.

Thus he appears to teem with information. He is, therefore, voluble, and didactic; sees everything in the light of an exhibition; and, like a showman, always wants an audience. Worldly in all his views, he is liberal with regard to sects; has no cavils on doctrinal points; usually conceals his prejudices; yields to circumstance; and declines or performs a ceremony with equal apathy. Sometimes for effect he sneers at the Greek images; laughs slyly at the picturesque figure of the bowing devotee; shrugs his shoulders as the priest goes by in his gloomy gown.

His morals depend on occasions; and, unlike Shakspeare's Angelo, he thinks it the same thing to be tempted, and to fall. He is bibulous, and rather courts than shuns "the invisible spirit of wine." He has an accumulative disposition; conspires, like some government contractors, with every one, against his employer; takes a surreptitious percentage on all the bargains which he makes for him; leads him about as if he owned him; excites his suspicions against the roguery of others, in order to conceal his own; constantly discredits the veracity of his own people, while he himself, like the Classic thieves, dedicates his tongue to the God of liars.

He avoids as much as possible all inconvenient duties; practices very little self-denial; expects regular wages; extra allowances at times; and when he leaves, valuable presents, and an unqualified testimonial to his virtues.

Such is the guide. After he is tired of his occupation, or has acquired by it all that it will yield him, he resorts to a settled life. He generally becomes a hotel keeper, and soon grows rich, respectable and oracular.

VIENNA.

We had a cold journey over the Brenner, the lowest of Alpine passes. We traveled the Tyrol, along valleys walled in by hills, wooded and cleared; by ravines deep and narrow, in which battles have been fought with rocks and bullets; over table lands dotted with cedar houses, which are at once both barns and dwellings, accommodating families and cattle. Women in short petticoats, red as their faces, and men in black buckskin breeches with bright buttons, toiled side by side in the fields; or harnessed with dogs and donkeys, dragged little carts.

We steamed down the Danube, whose banks sometimes spreading out into plains, are covered with villages; sometimes swell up into mountain cliffs, on which castles hang like eagles' nests. Here is a convent or chapel, famous for pilgrimages—there, the extensive chateau of a King or Count—there, the classic temple of Valhalla, filled with the busts of celebrated men.

We passed rafts of timber furlongs in extent—canal boats with towing horses by the score—whirlpools rushing with a noise like thunder—beautiful plantations and modern forts, and stopped at last in the Capital of the Austrian Cæsars.

The old Vienna, now the smallest portion of the city, is seated like an island, amongst the suburbs, surrounded by walls and trenches, and is entered on every side by bridges. It has fine old palaces, and numerous squares with fountains, statues, trees and pleasant walks.

The houses are all stuccoed, high and large, with families on different floors, and one sometimes contains the population of a village. By the great arched gateways, the porter with tinseled cap and shoulders, and a stick like a music major's, tells the visitor how many stairs to climb, and what bell to pull, to find his friend. Aristocracy is in the inverse proportion to the height of the occupant; and respectability declines as you ascend.

The streets narrow and roughly paved, diverge like rays from a central point. The sidewalks are almost imaginary. Drivers regard no division lines; and one is in constant proximity to carriages and horses, much to the peril of the short sighted, the absent minded and the hard of hearing. The gayest windows are stored with porcelain tobacco bowls and amber segar tubes; while all the shops are designated, not by owners' names, but by signs like taverns. You buy gloves at the "Golden Star," linen at the "Green Tree," coats of the last fancy at the "Silver Button," and patent hats at the "Lion's Head."

Museums and galleries abound. There are the starred green velvet robes, and the crown, with false stones, which Napoleon wore at Milan. The crown of Charlemagne with uncut jewels; and his Dalmatian shoes. The largest Opal, and the largest Cameo known. The ivory hilted sword of Tamerlane, and the silver gilt cradle of the King of Rome. A specimen of the gold of an Alchemist. Heavy meteoric fragments, some with dark sides, smooth as glass. The crimson standard of the besieging Turks. The stone battle axe captured from Montezuma by Cortez. Titian's "Ecce Homo." Reuben's "Jesuit casting out the devils." The "Holy Trinity" by Durer. "Teniers' Marriage of the Peasants." "The Helen" of Canova. "The Adonis" of Thorwaldsen. The curious parchment map of the Roman Empire in the fourth century. The Jerusalem delivered, written and interlined by Tasso's own hand.

There are various hospitals, gardens, and parade grounds. The royal remains are distributed amongst the churches—the heart in one, the entrails in another, anp the body in a third.

The Sabbath is a day of sport; and though some might be seen in the morning counting their beads at St. Stephen's; and some counting out change in their stores; yet by noon, the last prayer and the last penny have been made. The bells ring gaily; the organ grinders pull away at every corner; the bands play at the barracks; and there is music everywhere.

The walls are covered with attractive placards. There is a new actress—a new concert—a strange show. A foreigner plays in French tragedy. Strauss' company perform in the saloon at Sperls. A ball is open at Volksgarten. Fire-works are to be exhibited in the Prater. A constant holiday crowd is flowing towards the gates, the Glacis and the Bastions.

Nearly every one is affable and courteous. The men are continually lifting their hats in salutations. They uncover when they enter a shop; kiss when they are glad to see one another; wish their friends a good appetite when they eat; good luck when they sneeze, and a good voyage when they travel.

They are generally economical, ride mostly in third-class cars, and the forepart of steamboats. They breakfast in their bed-room on bread and black coffee; dine by the card at noon; and sup voraciously on sausages at twilight. They drink more beer than the English; and smoke more than Americans.

The Emperor, when I saw him some years ago, had the air of an innocent boy; his face showed neither intelligence nor beard. He walked in the evening along the promenade of his country seat—while the music and the fountains played—familiarly amongst his children, as he called his subjects, puffing a segar with juvenile vehemence.

His cabinet then was partly composed of men who had risen from the barricades, and become hostile to the very measures which placed them in power. The revolution of 1848, therefore, did not accomplish what it promised.

But it gave some freedom to the press. It opened the courts to the public. It gave criminals the right to a jury trial. It allowed a Legislature to be elected by an almost universal suffrage. These privileges have doubtless, been since qualified, and some of them withdrawn.

Even then the city wore the complexion of a camp. Cannon frowned in the open places. Bayonets gleamed at every turn. Swords rattled over the paving stones. The Judges presided in military dress. The palace was like a General's quarters in time of war. The extremities of the Empire were in a still more unsettled condition.

Since then, a disastrous foreign campaign has cut off a large portion of territory. Another internal revolution might overthrow a throne, still trembling from the shocks of the last.

BALLOONS.

The navigation of the air has been the puzzle of ages. Men have attempted it by infinite methods, but with only partial success. We read of Dædalus, soaring away in his fabulous flight from Crete, on his waxed wings—of the Wooden Pigeon of Archytas, made to float as was thought, by magic—of the Eagle constructed at Nuremberg, which flew out and saluted Charles the Fifth—of Roger Bacons' proposition to sail a globe with liquid fire—of Bishop Wilkins' plan to keep artificial wings in motion by a mainspring like that of a watch—of the contrivance of Francis Lana, to ascend by copper vessels exhausted of air—of De Gusman's machine with its hollow tubes, its bellows, its magnets and amber—and of others who lost their fortunes, their senses and their lives in fruitless efforts to fly like birds.

At last we find the Montgolfiers, less than a century ago, making the first balloon; and sending the fearless voyagers to the clouds by means of air heated by burning straw. Then soon afterwards, we hear of ascensions by hydrogen gas, for military and scientific objects; for amusement, and for livelihood. Latterly it has been quite common to see on Sundays, several of these ærial sailors floating over Paris.

While dining one afternoon in a restaurant, I was interrupted by the tramp and noise of persons running from all directions, down the Rue de la Paix. Expecting a fire, or a revolution, I hastened out, and saw two balloons nearly overhead, still at a great height, and one of them falling with fearful rapidity. Down it came, faster and nearer—now drifting horizontally in a current—then suddenly sinking. Once it appeared to drop like lead for a distance, then its descent for a time, was retarded. As it came lower, three persons were discovered in the car. Soon they were seen throwing out promiscuous articles. Cloaks, boots, shawls, handkerchiefs, hats, collars and a bonnet came tumbling and circling to the ground. Though somewhat checked they bore directly down against a church steeple. An appalling catastrophe seemed inevitable. The slightest contact must be fatal. The merest interference with the netting or the car, would disturb their equilibrium, and dash them to pieces. As the collision became imminent, and the intervening distance could be measured by yards and by seconds, the excitement below grew intense. Along the streets, and on the roofs of houses, men were frantic with emotion. But all were powerless; no advice could instruct, no courage or humanity could afford relief. The machine now careened within a handbreadth of the cupola. The next vibration must cause it to strike. People gasped for breath—some glanced another way to avoid the sight—some grew sick and swooned—some threw up their hands in a vain offer to save—some dropped their arms in despair—all were pale and dumb with terror. When just as the shock and crash of death were expected, a puff of wind made, perhaps, by the balloon's own motion, caused it to veer off—it swung gently away—down by the chimney stacks and cornices—and its living freight were saved. The crowd smiled with joy. The landing was made. A lady bareheaded, and two gentlemen in shirt sleeves and without hats or hose, still wearing the ghastly expression of their escape and danger, were soon overwhelmed with congratulations.

Having refreshed themselves in a cafe, two of them re-mounted the car, rose again rapidly; and relieved by their re-ascension, as was afterwards related, the anxiety of the father of one of them, who was in the other balloon.

Various novelties are sometimes introduced in these exhibitions to increase their attractions. Induced by a large handbill posted about Vienna, I followed the living stream that poured into the Prater, to witness a man go up on horseback.

It excited extraordinary curiosity. The wide field was covered with spectators. Mounted policemen, courteous and vigilant, were riding in all directions. Coaches garnished with heraldry moved along the avenues. Pretty women were strolling in full dress under the chestnut trees. Showmen were displaying their numerous wares and tricks at every turn. Hucksters were everywhere offering cakes, and fruit and beverage. All the men appeared to smoke either cigars, cigarettes or pipes.

The balloon with a zodiac painted on it, soon filled and began to rise. First was seen the man's head, which was a source of incipient satisfaction; and as he gradually appeared with the horse beneath him, sumptuously caparisoned, the admiration became boisterous; and a great shout greeted the gallant cavalier. But he neither bowed, nor moved a limb, nor spake a word, nor gave a sign of recognition. The horse's ears kept erect; his tail stood straight and permanent. A low murmur of surprise succeeded; then came an inquisitive pause; an instant's suspicion—and there was a simultaneous perception of the hoax. Twenty thousand people, as if they thought their credulity deserved deception, broke forth into a universal laugh—so loud and prolonged, that the air seemed shaking with merriment—as the irresponsible wooden æronauts sailed ludicrously away towards the stars.

It was on the Champ de Mars, of Paris, whence in 1780, the first hydrogen balloon went up, that I once saw a spectacle, which was unique even in that city of shows.

The population, from the rag-pickers to Napoleon, gathered there to behold the ascension of a chariot and horses. A wide circuit was formed, and inclosed by ropes to prevent intrusion. Bands of music enlivened the interval of preparation. Infantry, cavalry and uniformed police threw a military lustre over the scene. The balloon itself made of red, white and blue, represented the national colors. As it swelled out into its enormous globular dimensions, it seemed like a miniature planet about to be launched on its orbit.

Mr. Poitevin, his wife, and servant seated in an open four wheeled vehicle, drove the two ponies around the ring, amidst bravos and applause. This display showed that there was no imposition intended, and that there would be no interference by the Government. It had been said, that as the elevation of the animals would injure them, and cause the blood to gush from their nostrils, so cruel an experiment would not be allowed.

In the meantime, several small balloons were sent up in advance; some in the shape of men, painted in gaudy colors, and which retaining their upright position, went dancing over the city like real harlequins.

Presently, the long circuit having been made, the æronauts drove towards the great balloon—the horses halted—drew back—reared—and with some difficulty were attached to the netting, by straps placed under their bodies, and the bed of the wagon.

At the word—at a tap of the drum—with a stroke of the whip—and a bound of the horses, who vainly attempted to strike the ground—they suddenly rose as if at a gallop, amidst the applauding clamor of tongues and trumpets. But the poor beasts, as they saw the earth sinking beneath, hung their heads and tails in hopeless humility. For a long time the unscattered multitude gazed steadfastly and wonderingly at them, as they ascended above house tops—above steeples and towers—above the flight of birds. They drifted for a while, eastwardly, and then soared up till they diminished to half their bulk—till their outlines grew indistinct—till horses, wagon and æronauts faded into a point—till they disappeared beyond the reach of tubes and glasses.

The next morning the journals announced their safe descent and return to Paris. Afterwards I saw the same party make a successful ascent from the same place on three horses, one being elevated above the others, in a sort of pyramidal group. A feat which seemed to rival that of the enchanted steed of Walpole.

BERLIN.

Berlin is in the midst of a sandy plain, through which flows the Spree, an insignificant stream, called, by courtesy, a river. The streets well paved, well cleaned, wide and straight; brick houses stuccoed, uniform in style and color; numerous public buildings of architectural merit; some pleasant promenades; a beautiful fountain, and several national works of art adorning the gates, the bridges and the squares, give the city rather a magnificent appearance.

There is any amount of amusement for the idle, and every advantage for the studious. There is an elegant Opera house, where Tœchteck was the prima donna; and Taglioni danced in the ballets—and a theatre, where authors sometimes played in their own comedies; and Meyerbeer lead the orchestra in his own music.

The museum has its outside frescoed by Cornelius, with a representation of the dawn and progress of the world.—The first day, born amidst the smile of Hope and the songs of Angels; then the sports of shepherds; the reign of the Muses; the inauguration of Labor; the glory of Law. Within the building are pictures of all schools—some new, some rare—such as the famous piece of Leda and the Swan; and Io and the Cloud, once partially injured under a fastidious notion of propriety.

The attic of the Palace is full of curious relics—the tall mug from which Luther drank his beer; the cocked hat Napoleon wore at Waterloo; the canes and linen of Frederick the Great; the spangled uniform and stockings of Murat; the model windmill which the Czar Peter built in Holland.

The arsenal contains weapons of all eras, from the leathern cannon of Gustavus to the last invented gun and bullet. You may ride thence in a premium droskey, and draw, perhaps, a lottery prize; see sentinels presenting arms to an officer almost out of sight; and truck wagons hauled by curs, who run howling to the market, an open place without roof or stalls.

In an eating house you may have soup of apples, or of ale; drink beer in a wine cellar, noisy with the rattle of dominoes, and dark with tobacco smoke.

The widest street in Europe is here, planted with lindens through the centre; crowded with fashionable folks at noon; and until the watchmen whistle the hours at night, shining with windows full of iron trinkets and Dresden china. The Thiergarten is laid out in sandy walks amongst beech and cedar trees; where cripples play hand organs; and ladies with lap dogs, and officers off duty, lounge along the alleys.

An entertaining establishment, called Krolls, since burnt, was fancifully arranged with grottos; mossy rocks and gushing water-falls; sylph-like figures floating in the air; lamps glittering amongst lilies, and music which seemed to issue from the clouds. Near by, is a little lake, which, when frozen over, was daily ringing with the merry sound of skaters—boys and girls, old men and dames, went whirling and wheeling as if their heels were winged like Mercury's.

The churches are chiefly Protestant, but not heated in winter; and you may sit, and shiver, and listen there to noted theologian doctors, who are paid by the State; or, perhaps, see an ancient couple celebrating the golden marriage, by renewing the vows which they first made fifty years before.

The University has usually fifteen hundred students, who are allowed to smoke in the lecture rooms; and are called in their first year, foxes; in the second, lions; and in the last, asses.

While there, several years ago, I saw Humboldt at a society meeting; every one rose as he entered. He wore a dark suit and a white cravat. His expression was benevolent, as became one whose life had been devoted to the improvement of mankind. His head was large, and his forehead broad and high, as his genius was comprehensive and original. His keen, bright eyes, were such as one could fancy, had surveyed nearly all the visible globe. His white hair hung, like a silver crown, around his temples. The prestige of his learning, greater than Pliny's; and of his travels, more extensive than Plato's; and his imposing appearance, made one regard him with a sort of wonder, as the representative of a scientific century, and a great oracle of nature.

There also was Encke, who had give his name to a comet, engaged amongst lenses and logarithms; with his right eye larger than the left, owing, perhaps, to his ocular labors. There was Schelling, the head of a numerous school in metaphysics; Ranke and Raumer, the historians, both men of small stature. Heffter, Gneist and Keller, doctors of law; Dove, professor of physics; Muller, of anatomy; Lepsius, of antiquities; and Ritter, the geographer, who was very old and dressed in black stocking and knee breeches.

The funeral of Link, the botanist, was followed by the royal coaches.

The courts of justice had no rules of special pleading, and few books of reports. The Judges decided facts in civil cases; determined the law without regard to precedents; and the majority of a criminal jury could render a verdict. The two chambers of the Legislature were elected by restricted suffrage, under the constitution of 1848, which was so loosely or adroitly worded, that it did not prevent oppression.

Personal liberty was guaranteed—but in a time of peace, one could hardly move without permission of the police. The dwelling was inviolable—but under a pretext of public safety, every house was open to officials. The press was free—but a word against the administration was punished by banishment. Speech was free—but the people could not assemble in the open air for political discussion. The ministry was responsible—but it met an accusation by a dissolution of the chambers.

The King was amiable, fond of his wife, of literature and champagne—but he repented of the concessions forced upon him in 1848, and was anxious to recover his lost prerogatives. The Government tried every means to bring back the system which the revolution had partly destroyed. Thus they lost confidence at home; and afterwards, the respect of Europe, by their external policy.

The affairs of the Electorate of Hesse and of the Duchy of Holstein offered a fair opportunity to Prussia of becoming the defender of constitutional ideas. The sympathy of the world was with her, as she seemed to be preparing to oppose the oppressive interference of Austria, instigated by the Russian Czar.

She summoned her subjects, and they forgot the broken pledges and delayed reforms, and responded with enthusiasm. Old men had not seen the like. The whole nation became an 'army. From the fields, the shops and the lecture rooms, came the farmers, the tradesmen, and the students. Pamphlets were written on the ambitious designs of the enemy. The newspapers teemed with articles about Frederick the Great and the Fatherland. Ancient glory and ancient sacrifices were recalled. Striplings were reminded of those who bore the national eagles at Leipzig; and girls of their grandmothers, who had exchanged their jewelry for iron. Horses were taken from cabs and wagons to mount the cavalry. Tailors and women sewed day and night amongst brass buttons and blue cloth. The streets echoed with the continual rattle of artillery trains and kettle drums. The crown Prince reviewed the troops as they passed. The King harangued them on horseback.

There were parting scenes at the stations—mothers went to wring the hands of sons—young wives to weep at sudden separations—servant girls to exchange farewell-winks with corporals.

But all this proved to be a vain parade, a mere bluster, which signally failed of its purpose. The court of St. Petersburgh prevailed without a blow; its influence urged the Prussians out of the Electorate, and sent an Austrian army into the Duchies. Foreign powers smiled at the ridiculous conclusion of this bravado; but every honest Prussian blushed for his country.

A VISIT TO A GERMAN BARON.

One winter morning, as I was taking the usual Continental breakfast of biscuit and coffee, in the gayest cafe in Berlin, a middle aged, respectable looking gentleman came in, and sat near me. Perceiving that I read Galignani, a newspaper, printed at Paris, in English, and found in the principal coffee houses of Europe, he accosted me in that language.

He spoke intelligently of the topics of the day; the threatened war with Austria; the discipline of the Prussian troops, who had been marching for weeks through the streets; and the chief objects of interest in the city. When he discovered that I was from the United States, he became more cordial, and terminated the interview with an offer of friendship and hospitality. Giving me his address, he civilly invited me to his house. By his card, it appeared that he was Baron S., formerly an officer in the military service.

A week later, strolling along amidst a brilliant crowd of vehicles and pedestrians, in the Thier Garten, the fashionable promenade of the Prussian capital, I found myself opposite the residence of my titled friend. It was a handsome house, very high, and gave an impression of wealth and importance. The front door bell was rung without success. A wood-chopper, in a side alley, beckoned me to a back gate. I rang there, and a seedy servant directed me to ascend the stairway.

I journeyed up for five or six stories—every one of which was occupied by a family—until the Baron's door was reached, on the last flight of steps. It seemed as if I had climbed a mountain or a monument; and with some feeling of triumph, I stood upon the summit. Here, thought I, the Baron has some enchanting prospect which repays him for the toil of the ascent; or, perhaps, some eccentric humor which sees enjoyment in an inconvenience; or, perhaps, some malady which the exertion of climbing alleviates; or, perhaps, he is self-denying and mortifies the flesh for penance; or, perhaps, he rents his more convenient rooms below for the purpose of increasing his charitable funds.

Indulging such thoughts—and though his printed card was nailed on the door—I still expected to be dazzled by the costly appointments usually associated with rank. I was not unprepared for a display of liveried servants, tapestried walls, velvet floors and luxurious seats. A young boy—between a peascod and blossom, as Shakspeare says—in shirt sleeves and second-hand trowsers, both of which seemed spotted with dye stuff, admitted me into an uncarpeted parlor.

This shabby fellow, and the desolate appearance of the room, rather chilled my imagination. A piano, which seemed to be the relic of better days, stood alone in a dingy corner. A stove no larger than a man's hat, and used for cooking, had on it an earthen coffee pot, with a broken handle. The only chair had no back, which, after the warmest salutation, the Baron politely tendered to me, while he inclined against the window sill.

We had a desultory conversation about the news and his son, ten years of age, whose warlike disposition threatened my pantaloons with a tin sword; and which seemed to assure his father that he was destined for the navy. Nothing could be inferred from what he said, that he was in any way embarrassed; or that his present circumstances exhibited anything unusual. He regretted, unnecessarily, as the sequel proved, the absence of his lady, whose proficiency in music would have afforded an agreeable entertainment.

Suddenly a loud voice was heard at the door, and the desired lady entered at a bound. She was younger than her husband; with indifferent features; and rather carelessly attired in rusty garments. With eyes glistening like a panther's, she assailed the Baron with a volley of German. He deprecated her abruptness, and pointed imploringly towards me. But excited beyond control, she raged like a Fury, and made alarming gesticulations. The poor man at last exasperated, returned her abuse; and a universal hubbub filled the hospitable mansion.

The difficulty arose from the Baron's selling some mattresses, and keeping the money. I made a positive move to depart—the great lady observed me then for the first time; and with much courtesy requested me, as did also the Baron, to remain for dinner. Not being assured of a very long truce between the parties; nor tempted by the prospect of a luxurious repast, I thanked them kindly, and made a lively retreat. Ruminating, as I descended, on the happiness of high life above stairs, and the mysteries of German aristocracy.

HOLLAND.

There are but few countries which are more interesting than Holland. The sea has been driven from its bed to afford sites for cities, and fields for harvests. The tide is higher than the land, and the surf beats over the housetops. It requires constant labor to avoid disaster. All the hills are appropriated for dikes. Fire and winds are employed against the water. Banks composed of sand, straw, and twigs, and planted with grass and willows, form the roads, and fix limits to the ocean. Pumps, which are worked by sails or steam, bail out the leakage, and expose new soil. The country is intersected by canal and ditches.

The Hollander finds water wherever he turns—the first object in the morning—the last at night. Its vapors float over his head—its percolations form the bog at his feet. Its prevalence assails all his senses—he hears its roar beyond the dikes—he sees it around him in currents or in ponds—he smells its impurities at all hours. It pervades his cities, and his meadows.

It obviates, in a great measure the necessity of fences, roads, and forts. It divides his possessions from his neighbors—protects his property from trespass—defends his country from invasion. It supplies him with food for his table—a staple article for export—and facilities for transportation, travel, and amusement. In winter, on sleds and skates, he slides and glides upon its surface. He builds his summer house over the pool, to while away the sultry hours, amidst the croaking of frogs, the gambols of terrapin and the fumes of his pipe.

He sometimes makes a boat his home, and has a garden, cultivates vegetables, pigs, poultry, and children, amongst oars, ropes and canvas. The wharf streets are crowded with wharehouses, full of fish cured for commerce. It seems as if nearly every man is a sailor. The people indulge themselves in a holiday when the fishing smacks weigh anchor. Parties were once designated by the names of Hooks and Codfish. One of their greatest benefactors was Beukel, who discovered the method of pickling herring. Another was Roblas, who contrived the method of constructing permanent dikes. Another is asserted to have invented canal locks.

One of their best admirals was a fisherman. One of their best strategists inaugurated the policy of turning the sea through sluices against an enemy. It was the flood which delivered their beleaguered cities, when starvation and the Spaniards assailed them. It was their fleet which ravaged the coast, and humbled the flag of England. It was to save their ship from capture, that Van Speyk destroyed it, with himself and crew. It was by a bark of armed men concealed under fuel, that a Dutch Captain recovered Breda.

Thus the element, which invests Holland, is associated with its interest and its glory, with its history, with its hopes. It is at once the source of prosperity and danger. It is prominent in every description and caricature of travelers. It provokes the jest of wits, and the sneers of the splenetic. They have called the country the paradise of ducks and lizards—"a land that rides at anchor"—where the people are amphibious—where the women are descended from mermaids, and the men once wore fins.

But plentiful as is that fluid, it is in most places unpalatable, and one might say with the ancient Mariner:

> "Water, water everywhere,
> Nor any drop to drink."

They are often obliged to transport it from distant springs. They conduct into reservoirs all the rain that falls.

The facilities for washing, are however, so extensive, that scrubbing seems to be as much of a pastime as a duty. Cleanliness of a certain sort, is a national virtue. The floors are as white as lime, upon which, often, as upon those of a mosque, none but barefeet are allowed to tread. Yet frequently, the stable adjoins the dwelling, and the cow and the family enjoy the shelter of the same roof.

Politeness is very general. Peasants raise their hats to strangers—yet, nearly every man wears his hat in church, and burns his tobacco in the cars and the stations, though a notice in four languages forbids smoking.

Their customs are curious and permanent. As with the ancients, ivy leaves marked a wine shop: and Lucian's lawyer, to allure the clients, decked his gate with with twigs of palm: so badges are common here. Lace is fastened on the door when a child is born, and prevents the entrance of a bailiff. A basket of evergreens over a shop announces the arrival of fresh herring in the spring. A bulletin hanging from the knocker states the condition of an invalid, and saves him from intrusion. Images of turbaned Moors indicate the drug stores. Men dressed in black with cocked hats and wigs, knee breeches and stockings, are employed to announce a death, and attend a funeral. The stage drivers blow their horns at every village. The watchmen, with the prudence of Dogberry, give notice of their approach by striking the pavement with an iron staff.

The women look handsome and wholesome—ruddy with blood and health. They adorn their heads with caps, and bands of brass or gold. They carry with them wherever they go, a small basin of hot coals for their feet. They are not, however, entirely devoted to display. They hold the plough in the field. They haul the boat in the canal. They drag the truck to market, in the traces with a dog. They are sometimes obliged to hire their sweethearts for a festival.

The poor of both sexes wear wooden shoes. The houses are built of bricks or frame, and covered with tiles or thatch. They are sometimes very high; their gables face the street; and because of their yielding foundations generally lean a foot or more from the perpendicular. Storks live on the chimney tops; and some of them are maintained by the Government.

The steeples are as sharp as spears. The clocks chime the hours. The sidewalks are formed of brick laid edgwise. Mirrors are arranged outside of every window to reflect within the transactions of the street. The wheelbarrows have no legs. Coaches are seen on runners instead of wheels. The wagons are long, low and narrow, without tongues, and the driver guides them with his foot upon the pole. The traces are made of ropes. The ploughs have a prop to hold them steady. The clods are mashed with a shovel, not with rollers.

The cows in winter have their tails tied up. They paint the trunks of certain trees; and carve arches through the branches; and train the plants into curious shapes. They burn peat for fuel; they drink gin and beer for a beverage; and are almost the only Europeans who chew tobacco.

They encourage music—but their most common instruments are those which are filled by the bellows, or played by a crank. They are fond of those huge organ pipes, whose roar seems like thunder evolved in tunes—and of those vagrants with portable boxes, who huckster music on the highways. They have no singing boatmen like Venice. You do not hear Tasso's echoes on the water.

There seem to be but few fine specimens of architecture. Marble columns are not so numerous as the masts of vessels. The landscape displays more windmills than palaces. The museums, amongst other things, have curiosities from Japan and the ocean—delicate straw work, and pens of hair to write on sand—and mermaids formed of female skeletons and fishes tails. Galleries, teeming with pictures of hay fields, cattle, game and shipping, illustrate the practical genius of the people.

They are industrious. Trade is universal; and each town is distinguished for some particular branch of business. Deventer is devoted to the baking of ginger cakes, and the process is regulated by law. Gonda is famous for those tobacco pipes which seem to contribute so much to the phlegm and happiness of Dutchmen. Alkmaar is the chief depot for cheese, which is made round as cannon balls, and piled, like them, in pyramids upon the ground. Schiedam is the seat of those distilleries, whose aromatic schnapps give a charm to foreign drug shops.

Delft is the headquarters of the potteries. Haarlem is the market of flowers; where once the tulip mania raged, which afterwards infected Goldsmith, and reduced his fortunes to a shirt. Amsterdam is noted for cutting diamonds, and taking discount; and formerly sustained the armies, and controlled the currency of Europe. Rotterdam has had almost exclusive traffic with the Japanese; who so lately have, for the first time, traveled by railroad and read by gas light. Leyden, Gronigen, and Utrecht, have honored universities. The Hague holds the palace and the court.

All Dutch towns are delightfully shaded by trees. All have credit for their charitable institutions. Their patriots once assumed the name of beggars. Many of them have endured seiges as famous as those of Numantia or Genoa. Many of them are connected with illustrious names—with such statesmen as De Witt—with such scholars as Erasmus—with philosophers such as Grotius—with heroes like the Tromps—with painters like Rembrandt—with poets like Vondel—with Huyghens, who invented the pendulum clock—with Coster, who carved types on blocks before Guttemberg, of Mayence—with Beiling, who, a prisoner on parol, imitated the scrupulous honor of Regulus in his voluntary return to be buried in the ground alive.

THE RHINE.

For several weeks we were on the banks, or on the bosom of the Rhine. It was a cheerless season. The rough signs of winter still prevailed. There were the wild winds; the cloudy skies; the chilling showers, and the strong red current of the swollen river.

But the grander features of the country were conspicuous; and heights, chasms and crags were not concealed by the luxuriant screens of summer. The ground was desolate and dark, except here and there a speck of green, or an early flower peeped through the brush, like eyes through eastern veils. The last year's leaves hung like rags upon the naked oaks; and the plaintive notes of some stray birds disturbed the silence of the forests.

A variety of scenery, history and legends, gives peculiar interest to these shores. Without the mountainous banks of the Elbe; or the massy antiquities of the Nile; or the vast commerce of the Thames, there are yet mingled, in some degree, the attractions of them all.

There are populous plains, with their ploughed fields and leafless orchards; and monuments to heroes and to victories. There are the white walls of cities, with free ports and impregnable bulwarks; the seats of trade and learning; on the sites of Roman camps—roads the legions made; where some generals received the imperial purple; and some centurions were buried; and some benefactors born; where Diets were held, which filled and emptied thrones, and changed religious creeds.

There are volcanic heaps thrown up in antediluvian times, in all irregular masses, inclining and abrupt—abounding in useful minerals and medicinal waters, and pierced by ravines, through which rush tributary streams.

There are ancient structures, in ruins or restored; castles with towers, polygonal and round, crushed or crumbling, black with the marks of sieges and the mold of years.

There, robber chiefs defied the Burghers; warrior Bishops levied tolls; Electors applied the torture; the Kaisers had a palace; Dwarfs made mirth; Troubadors made music; and captive Kings were held in prison; and gallant Knights went forth in armour, against infidels and monsters, in the cause of beauty and the Cross, to rescue women and Jerusalem.

There, are the white cloistered fronts of Convents, built for monks or maids; to which distinguished Reformers, or high born ladies, fled from shame or danger; and which are now often used as magazines, or hospitals, for invalids or wines.

There, are chapels of all styles—tall Italian towers; old Saxon arches; grand Gothic choirs; steeples shaped like bells, or spears, or pears, built of trachyte, bricks and sandstone.

There, martyrs suffered; miracles were witnessed; pilgrims traveled; Templars worshiped; emperors were crowned.

There, is a monastery, ruined by a law suit; one filled with virgin's bones; and one holds the body of an envied minstrel, borne thither by fair damsels, whose hearts his songs had won.

On the sunny sides and summits, amongst cliffs and crevices, on artificial terraces, covered with made soil, stuck like peas, hang the vineyards of the Rheingau —the Bacchanalian gardens—the source of those voluptuous liquors, which inspire more than love or landscapes.

There, are the places to which tradition has assigned facts and fables—where dragons were slain, and unseen spirits wander; houses which they say the devil curiously built; and fearful ladders, which he dug in the stone, to climb the precipice; the Seven Rocks, once seven cruel sisters, who would not wed, and whose bodies became as stony as their hearts; where perished the Baron's daughter, like Jeptha's, the victim of a vow; where the Brothers slew each other, made foes and lovers by one woman's smile; where the Royal hermit wasted hours and hopes, watching the windows of his monastic mistress; where the treacherous nymph, with the Syren's echo, allured the sailors to the whirlpool and the rocks; where the vermin devoured the wicked Priest, who betrayed the poor; where Constantine beheld the cheering vision of the Cross in heaven; and where Cæsar traversed the river on his ingenious bridge, against the fair-haired Germans.

Then, there are little vallies, with villages surrounded by crazy ramparts, equally dangerous to friend and foe; and quaint old gateways, with loopholes for the arrows, and the warders; and odd shaped houses built of brick, in wooden frames, whose opposite stories project till they almost meet, making the streets resemble tunnels.

In these close towns, and not in solitary cottages, the peasants live, for safety and from custom. They possess small tracts of land, often mortgaged to every grain of dust and blade of corn; which yet makes them freer than their ancestors, who rather belonged to the soil, than owned it.

The young girls, called madchens, with red round cheeks, and parrot toes, and sky blue eyes and stockings, were toiling amongst the vines; or on the way to market, or to mass; with baskets, or white muslin or silver caps upon their head; and silver daggers in their hair.

And thus, as we passed along this famous stream, by puffing steamboats, and through floating bridges, these various objects, by the way, recalled the dramatic scenes of history.

We beheld in fancy, Druids and Augurs encouraging hostile nations—Battles waged with javelins and arrows—The triumphant progress of disciplined invaders—The avenging victories of Barbarian hordes—The donwfal of a colossal empire—The fanatical march of the Crusades—the romantic incidents of Chivalry—The subtle discussions of the Schoolmen—Guttemberg exhibiting his wooden types—Luther before the Imperial diet—The expiring struggle of Feudalism—And, at last, the blooming glories of the new civilization burst upon the sense.

So, in the storied waters of the Rhine, one may read, as in some magic stereoscope, the great successive steps of human progress.

"PARLA."

Donatello to the Statue.

A distinguished public officer, and a few of his friends, wished Col. J., while on his Northern tour, to visit their Borough.

The officer and a large suite accompanied the Col. to the town of N., where the former had requested Mr. M., then a student, to meet them.

M.'s mission was not clearly defined.

However, on the appointed day, a two-horse coach and driver were ready for him; and as the autumn sun glistened on the white frost and the crimson forest—and the robins were circling round, preparatory to their annual flight—and the fox hounds were filling the land with their exciting cry—he was driven rapidly towards his destination.

Along the route, he speculated about the character of his office. He was not going for the mere purpose of taking the vehicle across the country, for that the driver could have done without him. He was not a messenger, for he carried nothing. He was not a committee, for he represented no assembly, public or private. He was not a delegate, for he had no instructions, expressed or implied. He concluded, therefore, that he was only a favored guest.

In a few hours, the wheels rested before the designated Inn. It was crowded by a variety of people—irrepressible boys—irresponsible men—votaries of wine and war, a few of whom seemed affectedly polite and mirthful; while the smoke and spittle of tobacco, the vapors of grog and powder, the flash of swords and glasses, and the noise of kettle drums, cannon and huzzahs, gave an anniversary aspect to the scene.

"Here he comes," said several voices as the coach door opened. "Here he comes" was passed from mouth to mouth, through the bar-room, up stairs, and down into the kitchen, and echoed back again, followed by a rush of people towards the new arrival, as, in a long, black cloak, he mounted the steps of the porch.

The officer, referred to, welcomed him with both hands. At his military voice the living sea, of soldiers and loafers, parted before the advancing procession of two persons abreast.

Having crossed the threshold, the officer spirited him behind a door. In a low tone he told him that he must rest a few minutes, and afterwards make a short speech to the Col. Then, as he hurried away, he warned him with an impressive motion of his finger, not to be agitated!

In spite of this concluding advice, and strenuous efforts to comply with it, M. was rather nervous. The time to be "wise and amazed," to be composed and inspired, seemed inadequate for the purpose.

The circumstances were sudden, the occasion novel, the audience large, and the opportunity for making a debut, so fair, that he was bewildered by conflicting impulses. He was unprovided with those general topics which the old rhetoricians advised for emergencies; and he was ignorant of that artificial stimulant which a subsequent authority recommended for the dumb. A rabble of thoughts in all disorderly associations passed through his mind.

His laboring imagination at last took a homeward flight. His subject loomed up in fair proportions. His ideas began to take shape and color. He beheld afar the ancient Borough arrayed in unusual attractions. It seemed like a town of temples and trees, of colonnades and domes, of spacious ways and wandering walks—where men wooed the arts, and surveyed the the planets, and tried the earth in crucibles—where emblematic colors, stirring music, persuasive tongues, and women's tears sanctified the patriotic aspirations of the living, and the heroic memories of the dead.

While he was enjoying this pleasant vision, and dreaming of rare applause and blushing honors, the officer returned. His growing confidence began to abate on his being immediately urged into a thronged room. At one end of it, in a dazzling red vest, surrounded by men with swords and feathers, stood the venerable dignitary he was expected to address.

But the Col.'s presence was not imposing. His figure was what is called square; and his features, without being unpleasant, were rugged and care worn.

As M. approached him, he raised his open hand, as if about to salute, or embrace him, while at the same time he said to the officer: "Ah! this is the young gentleman of whom you spoke so kindly."

This was an embarrassing compliment; as it seemed to make it doubtful whether the Col. anticipated anything but an introduction. It induced M. to advance too near for a speech, and yet not close enough to shake hands.

A pause ensued—as painful as the lover's before he proposes; as the duellist's before he fires; as the culprit's before he swings.

The drums ceased—the guns were silent—the cheers were withheld—the audience, after the usual preparatory buzz, became still—they listened—they looked. Yet they did not manifest the pious composure of a congregation; nor the restless anxiety of a stump meeting; nor the stoic indifference of a jury.

But they showed an earnest, patient curiosity, as if they yearned to hear, and expected to be pleased—" as if they supposed that all speakers commenced with difficulty—as if the hesitation only increased their confidence in his powers—as if they imputed it to the fervor of his emotions, or the affluence of his thoughts—as if they were whispering—"Look! he is winding up the watch of his wit, by and by it will strike!"

As the delay was prolonged, some raised themselves on chairs, to overlook those in front. Some put their hands to their ears, lest a syllable should escape. Some unconsciously opened their mouths, as if they would inhale the articulate breath.

Thus they waited with all the senses vigilant. But still no accents fell, no periods flowed.

The unfortunate proximity of the student to the Col.; the marked attention; the universal gaze dismayed him. He distrusted his ability to satisfy the expectation. He feared to take the responsibility of disappointing it. His mind vacillated. His thoughts wandered. His visions faded. Forsaken of all the inspirations; abandoned by every extempore god—he forgot his subject—forgot his errand—lost his consciousness—lost his voice—his own breath seemed to choke him—he could not utter a word—he could not open his lips—his eyes drooped—his feet shuffled—his hands twitched—he was eloquent only with pallor and perspiration—he was oratorical only in his tremor—he represented nothing so well as silence.

Before he could recover, the officer alluded to, restive and despairing, adroitly assumed his place, and performed his task. And while some smiled, and some wondered at the failure—a few naively called it a maiden speech!

LOUIS NAPOLEON.

Passing one day an entrance of the Palais de l'Elysee, the gates suddenly flew open, the two sentinels presented arms, a few people waiting there, fell back, and Louis Napoleon, the President of France, with an Aid by his side, and two liveried servants behind, drove through, in a light open wagon. He then halted for a moment to receive the numerous petitions which were offered to him. I saw him afterwards, as he got out of a plain carriage and went up to the American reading room, on the Boulevard. And again, on horsback, with a star on his breast, wearing a frock coat and cocked hat, in the midst of a brilliant group of officers of various nations, going to the Champ de Mars, to review the sham fight of twenty thousand soldiers on a side, arranged to honor the visit of the Lord Mayor and Aldermen of London.

He was rather below the ordinary height; his nose prominent; his eyelashes long; his glance steady, but downward, like the first Napoleon's; his moustache heavy and dark, shading his mouth. His face was impressive—calm, passionless, thoughtful and inscrutable; neither repelling by pride, nor attracting by sympathy; betokening a genius not to be seduced or daunted, but leaving it in doubt whether his instincts were good or evil.

His career shows how persistently he pursued a great object—how implicitly he relied upon his fortune. His birth in a palace—celebrated by the peal of cannon—his childhood associated with historical spectacles—bearing a name synonymous with military glory—inheriting pretensions favored by popular affection and tradition, his chief ideas and emotions were of crowns and armies.

Disappointment only instructed his ambition. The bitter ridicule, the personal perils and hardships with which inopportune efforts oppressed him, gave him patience and discretion. In all circumstances, as a student or adventurer, as soldier or constable, in sympathy with the aristocracies or the masses, amongst the Carbonari of Italy or against the Chartists in London, an exile in America, a citizen in the free canton of Thurgau, capitally arraigned before the tribunal of France, suffering the penal solitude of the dungeon of Ham, persecuted, punished, or feasted, he never doubted or despaired of his imperial destiny.

It was his study, his dream, his faith. It filled his imagination and sustained his spirit. It inspired the ingenious books which he wrote, the eloquent speeches which he delivered, his reticent deportment which baffled speculation, and made him a hero even to his familiars. It caused him to be indifferent to danger, and forbearing of provocation. It gave him that equanimity which neither the grenade of the assassin, the fire of battle, the flattery of parasites, nor the scorn or applause of multitudes could move. It accounts for his rashness and his prudence, his inconsistencies and his success.

If he was moderate or audacious—if he complained of suspicions or verified them—if he lauded free institutions in his progress through the provinces, and silenced the press and the tribune— if he arrested generals, and employed the army against the barricades of St. Antoine—if he dissolved the National Assembly, and appealed to universal suffrage, it was under the impulse of that feeling which, he said, made power essential to his existence.

Having attained the throne, he sought at once to justify his mission. He gave a spur to civil enterprise —infused energy into every branch of industry—offered prizes to ingenuity in the arts and sciences—covered the land with railways and machines—opened magnificent avenues through the cities—relaxed the rigor of restraining laws—distributed his purse amongst the the sufferers from inundations—invoked popular patriotism to sustain his treasury by voluntary loans—improved the efficiency of his artillery and ships with new weapons and new armor—perfected harbors and bulwarks on the coast—won laurels and territory in his campaigns—and established a personal prestige and influence rivaling his uncle's, greater than any living ruler's.

His conduct has become a constant subject of discussion and apprehension. A journey across the channel, a letter to an aid-de-camp, a sentence in the *Moniteur* a quasi official pamphlet, or an abrupt remark to an ambassador—and the stocks depreciate in the market, and the din of hostile preparation echoes over the Continent.

England, hitherto the haughtiest enemy of his house, does not move without his concurrence. Russia, with all her gigantic strength, still endeavors to avoid giving him offence. Germany beholds in him a continual menace. Italy would fain hail him as a deliverer. The Pope leans reluctantly on his support. The Sultan gladly dispenses with his aid in Syria. Spain humbly plays the role he assigns her. Mexico abhors, but unaided, may not decline his Grecian present of a king. The American Republic, in her trials, impatiently endures his marked disregard of her traditional jealousy of European interference on the western continent. All recognize his importance—none comprehend the breadth of his designs.

Powerful in resources, cautious in his means, abiding his time, keeping his counsels, a fatalist in feeling, profound in policy, systematic in combination, resolute and rapid in execution—he appears the most imposing figure of the age. And as he stands, in his mysterious attitude, on the borders of a transitionary civilization, affecting, it is said, some of the symbols of the ancient Cæsars, imbued with the Napoleonic notion of the confederacy of nations, and the consolidation of crowns—one is disposed to believe that his full proportions are not yet developed—that he has not yet reached his historical maturity—that he may yet be a signal actor in the great apocalyptic drama of the world.

THE CRYSTAL PALACE IN LONDON.

The press, the criers, the people, wending their way towards Hyde Park, gave notice of the last week of the great exhibition.

The edifice was wonderful!—so rare, so light, so strong, so large, so brilliant in its contents, so sudden in its rise, so soon to vanish!

Men had read of nothing like it in prose, or verse. It was all of glass or iron—columns, balusters, walls and roof. It covered eighteen acres of land; and old forest trees waved their green tops beneath its transparent arches. It stood unshaken by the fury of summer storms, and the undulating weight of moving masses. Individual genius, royal influence, and national enterprise had furnished it with all the curiosities they could discover or contrive. A year before, children had gathered violets on its unbroken sward; and a year thereafter, they played on the vacant spot, where it had held a world in minature.

On the day before its final close, one hundred and twelve thousand souls, from all regions, spread along its aisles, transepts and galleries. No disorder, no ribaldry, no petulance occurred. Good humor and good will prevailed. But an incident disturbed, for a while, the monotonous calm.

Several policemen were observed surrounding a person. Others hurried towards them, to ascertain the cause. The mass increased, and became impenetrable. The cry of "pickpocket" was raised and repeated. It aggravated the excitement. Hundreds, actuated by the common curiosity to see shame or crime, pushed forward.

The thousand usual incoherent questions and answers were passed. The arrest became the temporary topic of conversation. The police were praised for their dexterity, their usefulness, their importance. The English felt proud of this very public example of their vigilance.

Some related how the thief was caught. That he was an old convict—the officers knew him—saw him enter—one of them, in plain clothes, watched him—lounged carelessly in his way, tempted, and entrapped him. Every body was gratified at the result, for every body rejoices at retribution.

In the meanwhile a space was cleared in front of the individual who was the object of these remarks. He was an old man, dressed in a blue tight body coat; and his head drooped on his breast. A murmur of surprise instantly broke forth, as those near discovered that the police, instead of restraining an offender, were merely protecting from the pressure, no less a person than the Duke of Wellington.

The scene became somewhat grand, as the fact was made known; and as that heroic brow bowed, not in confusion, but with years and honors, and in courteous recognition of the cosmopolitan applause which greeted him. It seemed as if the representatives of all lands, and the huzzahs of all languages united, to pay the personal tribute of the age to one of its most illustrious characters.

On the next day, a less, but more select crowd entered the building, to take a farewell view of an exhibition, which had had no precedent; and which might never be repeated.

Some loitered around the cornices, the capitals, the the statues, the pictures, to admire how art had caught, as it were, the formative skill of nature, and forged her loveliest lines and richest colors.

Some looked over those personal articles of dress and toilet, whose materials grow on the back of brutes, and on the breast of birds; which the worm spins, and the flowers distil; which crystalize in the mine, and bloom on the savannas.

Some examined those successful arrangements of mechanical powers, which tend to diminish physical labor; and prepare society for a more intellectual development.

Some glanced at those fearful instruments of destruction, which seemed as if they would drive Mars, himself, in terror, from the field.

Some stood where the fountains spouted, through tubes, and over urns, of glass, to enjoy their refreshing spray, their murmuring fall, their changing tints.

Some gathered near the flowers, to behold the curious growth of that royal leaf, which inspired the architectural design of the great structure itself.

Some were entertained by the diversity of languages —by the softness of those of classic origin; by the sonorous Teutonic accents; by the guttural sounds of Orientals.

Some amused themselves with noting the numerous costumes—the flowing robes, the pointed caps, the plaited kilts, the lace, and tinsel.

Some studied the facial angles, the formal beards, the figures, and the manner of different races.

Some listened with delight to the gentle tones of musical instruments, as now and then, a cunning hand swept their harmonious chords.

Some admired the contrasted styles of living beauty—the blushing fulness of Rubens—the delicate grace of Correggio—the fascinating sadness of Guido—the passionate brightness of Titian—the heavenly innocence of Raphael.

Some passed along chatting of business or of news, seemingly unconscious of the vast show they had come to visit.

Some resting on the sofas, which were here and there distributed, regarded the spectacle as significant of the approaching fraternization of sects and tribes—as the emblem of that promised period in which guilt and pain shall flee away, and peace assumes her universal crown—

"Ac toto surget gens aurea mundo!"

But as the appointed hour drew nigh, other considerations yielded to the interest of the closing scene. The swaying heads, the tramping feet, the busy conversation ceased. Every eye was directed towards the transept galleries. The four corners were filled with choristers. Musicians were posted near with their instruments. The vast assembly stood up. The men took off their hats. The eager faces and subdued breathing, showed deep emotion. Then burst forth that noblest psalm of praise. A hundred singers led; a score of organs accompanied; forty thousand voices swelled the chorus. The mighty concert pealed along the crystal walls—resounded above the clangor of the city—the heavens, till then overcast, as if in sympathy, began to clear—the slanting sun-beams flashed far and high upon the breaking clouds—and the soaring splendors of the bow of peace responded to the doxology of nations.

OLIVER GOLDSMITH.

How charmingly Goldsmith wrote! whether of fact or of fiction, in poetry or prose! Whether he described a planet or a people, the peculiarities of genius, or the habits of a brute, the vicissitudes of life, or the features of a landscape!

He gathered contributions from science, and gave new interest to the phenomena of nature. He threw an attractive light down the fading aisles of the past, and over the wrecks of systems, customs and creeds. Delighted we climb with him the highest Alps, and see amongst the hundred realms below how appropriately all places and all people have been blessed. We wander with him over the desolate site of lovliest Auburn, to behold how the aristocracies of rank and fortune absorbed the privileges, and invaded the happiness of the poor; or around the shrubbery of the Vicar's cottage, to mark how constant virtue triumphs over adventitious ills; or through the great city, to enjoy the diversions of the drama, the streets, or the club.

His compositions are remarkable for purity of language, and apposite imagery, for ingenious reflections, soothing pathos, and unfailing humor. He has nothing obscure, affected, puerile or pernicious; yet he has both energy, and ornament. There is a tenderness in the melody of his verse; a pleasing cadence in his prose;

a sort of fascination in his descriptions; a fine philosophy in his sentiments. A spirit of benevolence chastens his style, warms his praise, softens his censure, and sheds a glow of moral beauty over all his productions.

His imagination, gay rather than brilliant, represents the humbler walks of society, familiar scenes, and sensible objects; employs no ideal agencies, and appeals to the gentler emotions.

His fictions are crowded with agreeable pictures and lessons. Extravagant incidents and characters are almost overshadowed by the propriety of other parts, or half redeemed by some special merit of their own. We enjoy the marvelous delusions in one piece—we sympathise with the wholesale misery in another—nor are we displeased by the rare instances of improbable disguises, incompatible duties, and unaccountable motives. They occasion the introduction of an elegant metaphor, a fine period, or a facetious point; or exhibit an amiable passion; or impress a wholesome truth. And while most of his men and women are fairly drawn, a favorable feature pervades the worst. His knaves, not always incorrigible, are apt to repent, or be useful; and his dupes, hardly ever desperate, affect us by their innocence: the first may excite our compassion—the latter elicit our fondness.

His humor is conspicuous in recounting mistakes, and social offences. He finds in defeated vanity, in unfounded pretensions, in confiding ignorance, in whimsical acts, and absurd fashions, those harmless incongruities which surprise us into mirth.

Hence his ridicule though keen, is not of the bitter sort; his shafts are pointed but not poisoned. He rarely plays upon words, or violates the canons of good taste. He is therefore not a punster like Hook; nor cynical like Swift; nor indelicate like Rabelais; nor profane like Voltaire. Yet he sounds with skill all the strains of pleasantry. Sometimes with the gentlest touch of Lamb; sometimes with the graceful ease of Addison; sometimes with the bolder strokes of Cervantes.

How ludicrous appears the confusion of his strolling, player, when the callous crowd reflect the disdainful silence of the London critic; and the dismay of the fond mother, when the overrated Moses unpacks his illusive bargains; and the family procession, with their unwilling steeds and unwitnessed finery, too tardy for parade or prayers; and the artful Jenkins, with his charitable face, beguiling the "glorious pillar of unshaken orthodoxy" of his wall eyed horse.

How well he entertains us with the story of the venison, with the masterly analysis of his literary friends, with the unthinking generosity of Honeywood; the overreaching cleverness of Constance; the mischievous ignorance of Tony; the abounding hospitality of Hardcastle; the unconscious impudence of Marlow; the racy gossip of Dame Quickly's ghost; the foppish swagger of Beau Tibbs.

And he constantly pours forth a felicitous current of droll expressions and ideas, which move the cheerful feelings, relax the muscles, make the eyes twinkle, wreathe the face with smiles, or shake the sides with laughter.

Contrasted with this sportive manner, is the plaintive beauty of his numbers. His flowing recital of the wrongs of pride, and pains of love, of vanished figures, sports, and years—his visions of the silent haunts of buoyant youth, of the vacant seats of hoary age, of landscapes dotted with ruins and with graves, inspire the mind with that tender melancholy, which subdues but does not darken it—which interests the virtues, im-improves the life, and shows that

"Our sweetest songs are those that tell of saddest thought."

If we turn from the author to the man, we find a character made up of curious whims, transient vices, and prominent traits of excellence. Every page in his biography is marked by some strange predicament in which his caprice or folly placed him.

That he was the son of a preacher, and born in Ireland, and died a bachelor, will account in the estimation of a few, for most of his oddities, his wit, his blunders, and for his leaving behind him a debt of several thousand pounds.

Occasionally, his simplicity might remind us of the pedagogue in Hierocles; and his poverty, of the ghost in Lucian, whose want of an obolus astonished Charon. His eccentricities commenced in his youth, and clung to him through life.

He secretly left college, paid his passage to America, and forgot to go aboard the vessel. He started for London to study law, and gambled away, in Dublin, his funds for the journey. He went to Edinburg to attend the medical lectures, and soon lost the place in which he had taken lodgings. He set out for Leyden, and sailed for Bordeaux. He borrowed money to travel, and spent it on tulip roots. He began his continental tour with one penny and one shirt. He wrote letters without dates; mistook a footman for a nobleman; a bailiff for a steward; an inn for a dwelling; and intending to compliment a lord, uttered a sarcasm. He was more than once arrested for debt, and once imprisoned in mistake for an agent of France. He often procured his dinner by arguing a thesis before an university; and his bed, by playing a flute before a cottage. At times he was an usher, at times a chemist, at times a physician, at last an author.

Though improvident and careless, he was vain of his own powers, and envious of the success of others. It vexed him that the King had conversed with Johnson; that people applauded puppets in his presence; and admired his lady companions more than himself. He renounced the friendship of Kelly, because he was the author of a play more popular than his own. He assaulted Evans, the printer, for his published strictures.

Though his figure was ungainly, and his face pitted with small pox, he dressed himself in gay colors, and ambitiously paraded in the Temple gardens. Though he was a poor talker, he attempted to shine in conversation. Though he was confused in the company of men of rank, he boasted of his interview with the Earl of Northumberland; and complained of the cold salutation of Lord Camden. He was unduly mortified at the moderate success of one of his comedies; and unduly elevated by the triumph of another.

These foibles were, however, not strong enough to enfeeble his mind, or infect his heart. They were but temporary in their influence, and his judgment condemned, and his candor confessed them. His merits predominated. He was found of children; he would give his last penny to the poor; he recommended others for favor when he needed it himself; he never degraded his pen; he never put his conscience in the market.

He had many qualities which rendered him fit to confer and enjoy social good. He had a pliant, cheerful, and forgiving temper. His manners were artless; his sensibility delicate and discriminating; his observations acute and extensive. He gathered information from all sources; found

> "Sermons in stones,
> Books in the running brooks, and good in every thing."

Without egotism he infused his own experience into his writings; and amused us with his errors. He was himself "The Good Natured Man;" the Tutor, in his novel; "The Traveler," and "The Man in Black."

Like his own description of Cumberland, he seemed as if

> "Vainly directing his view
> To find out men's virtues, and finding them few,
> Quite sick of pursuing each troublesome elf,
> He grew lazy at last, and drew from himself."

His mental powers, harmoniously disposed, were employed to impart knowledge, to refine the taste, and improve the virtues of society. "His poetry," said Fox, "was the best in the language;" "It represented the majesty of sensible philosophy," said Madame de Stael; "He was a great man," said Johnson; "He did all things happily," said Coleridge.

It has been more than a century since he lived. Of the various illustrious names which enrich the history of his time—though the dominant genius of Johnson shone like the centre of an intellectual system—though

Burke and Fox were about reviving the golden age of oratory—though Gibbon was preparing that massive work, whose irreverent irony alone impairs its splendor—though Collins was singing his beautiful ode to the passions—though Young was showering forth his thoughts, rich as pearls—though Churchill and Hogarth were exciting London by their satirical battles in verse and pictures—though Reynolds was shedding the graces of scholarship over his favorite art—though Quin, Foote, and Garrick, night after night, were moving crowds to tears and merriment by the exhibitions of the stage—though Sir Wm. Jones was developing those treasures of oriental learning which had been so long hidden from the European world—yet none of them—however gifted, or however praised, whatever his influence, or his labors—is more frequently, or more fondly mentioned than Poor Goldsmith.

www.ingramcontent.com/pod-product-compliance
Lightning Source LLC
Chambersburg PA
CBHW022026240426
43667CB00042B/1205